Advanced
English–Arabic Translation

Advanced
English–Arabic Translation

A Practical Guide

El Mustapha Lahlali and Wafa Abu Hatab

EDINBURGH
University Press

© El Mustapha Lahlali and Wafa Abu Hatab, 2014

Edinburgh University Press Ltd
The Tun - Holyrood Road, 12(2f) Jackson's Entry, Edinburgh EH8 8PJ

www.euppublishing.com

Typeset in Times New Roman by
Servis Filmsetting Ltd, Stockport, Cheshire
and printed and bound in Great Britain by
CPI Group (UK) Ltd, Croydon CR0 4YY

A CIP record for this book is available from the British Library

ISBN 978 0 7486 4584 8 (hardback)
ISBN 978 0 7486 7796 2 (webready PDF)
ISBN 978 0 7486 4583 1 (paperback)
ISBN 978 0 7486 7798 6 (epub)

Contents

Acknowledgements

We would like to express our gratitude to all those who have made this book possible. We wish to thank first and foremost our colleagues at the University of Leeds and at Zarqa University for their support and encouragement. We are deeply indebted to our families for their support and assistance throughout the writing stages of this book. Our special thanks go also to our friends for their encouragement and support.

Our sincere thanks also go to Dr Jalal Aldoseri for his valuable comments on a draft of this book.

Using this Book

The need for translation from English into Arabic and vice versa has grown substantially since 9/11 and the war on Iraq in 2003. Such a need has increased demands for translation services from and into these two languages. Unfortunately, the educational market has suffered from a lack of textbooks that address translation from a practical point of view, taking into consideration the changing nature of the translation market on social, economic and political levels. Translation is a highly demanding process that involves much more than utilising and converting words and phrases from one language into another, and translators and learners need a practical book that addresses the skills and sub-skills of translation: this book is designed to address some of these needs.

This book introduces learners to translation from English into Arabic through a wide range of practical exercises. With a variety of texts and multiple drills, it is hoped that learners will be able to develop and refine their translation skills. The book introduces learners to drills related to the translation of texts within basic genres, and covering translation sub-skills. It aims to present an efficient and practical approach to learning the skills of translating different text types from English into Arabic. Whilst most of the published translation books tend to focus on the theoretical aspects of translation from the source text (ST) to the target text (TT), this book follows a practice-based approach in order to assist learners in utilising the concepts and theoretical frameworks they have learned. Some theoretical aspects of translation are introduced in the first four modules, but readers are urged to consult other books that elaborate at length on these theoretical aspects.

As well as offering advanced materials for translation from English into Arabic, the book also includes a wide range of drills pinpointing the differences between the source language (SL) and the target language (TL) so that learners and translators can refresh their knowledge of some aspects of the TL.

Not only will the book be useful to those learners who wish to familiarise themselves with the different typology of Arabic and English texts, it will also equip them with some necessary translation skills. Furthermore, the book introduces students to general translation skills by focusing on specific technical texts that require certain 'detective' skills, which students learn through the practical drills offered on each text. These drills are designed to help learners progress through the word level, sentence level and discourse level. Since context is at the heart of translation, students are introduced to a variety of drills that allow them to translate different elements of discourse in their appropriate context.

It is hoped that the practical drills will enhance learners' skills in selecting appropriate equivalence to the ST, especially in the translation of technical texts. In addition to mastering knowledge of both languages, translators need to have a good command of specific registers, some of which will be acquired through specialised dictionaries, encyclopaedias and technical literature in both languages. In order to facilitate learners' comprehension and translation of texts, a glossary of some technical words and phrases is provided at the end of each text. On completing this book, learners should have acquired technical vocabulary at an advanced level, further enhancing their ability to translate from English into Arabic.

All in all, this book is intended to improve and strengthen learners' translation skills, and refine and expand their knowledge of different genres of texts. The main objectives can be summarised as follows:

1. introducing learners to the main features of different genres of texts
2. identifying the linguistic and cultural features of different text types
3. equipping learners with the necessary skills to deal with the translation of different genres of texts from English into Arabic, through practical translation drills
4. enhancing awareness of pragmatic, semantic and sociolinguistic aspects during the translation process.

Key to Symbols

 Glossary

 Translation

Structure of the Book

This book is composed of seven modules. The first four modules examine various aspects of translating different genres into Arabic. A range of drills then follows, which are designed to help learners digest these concepts. Modules 5, 6 and 7, however, are more practical. They offer drills and exercises to help students practise some of the theoretical concepts introduced in Modules 1, 2, 3 and 4, and apply them to different text genres. With this in mind, each module starts with an overview of the genre in question and is followed with drills and exercises to help learners practise the translation strategies outlined. Before they are tackled in detail, Module 1 will cover the common strategies of translation in order to acquaint learners with the various ways they can translate their texts.

The modules are:

1. Foundation Methods of Translation
This module introduces students to some of the main translation approaches and frameworks that students would find useful in translating different texts. These approaches are not comprehensive but representative of the main translation approaches used in the field.

2. Literary Texts
This module introduces students to literary texts and literary translation from English into Arabic, covering poetry, fiction and drama. Characteristics of each type of literary text are illustrated along with translated examples, mainly from English into Arabic.

3. Economics Texts
This module deals with the translation of texts on economics and finance as well as other issues dealt with in business language.

4. Scientific Texts
This module deals with the translation of scientific texts in areas such as medicine, physics, chemistry and psychology. Learners are shown how to deal with scientific discourse using the appropriate terminology and linguistic structures.

5. Media Texts
This module introduces the learner to a range of media texts. The main objective is to allow learners to familiarise themselves with the media register and to refine their translation skills. The module also introduces the main features of media texts.

6. Administrative Texts
Modules 6 and 7 are related. This module introduces students to administrative texts and provides learners with glossaries to help with their translation of texts in this genre.

7. Legal Texts

This module introduces learners to the main features and characteristics of legal texts including civil law documents, business contracts, court documents and orders, international legal documents and resolutions, civil partnership documents, international treaties and conventions. A general introduction to the main features of legal texts, as well as the challenges of translating within this genre, is also provided.

Map of the Book

Module and Topic	Translation Methods and Strategies	Genre	Translation Exercises	Translation Problems
Module 1: Foundation Methods of Translation	Methods of Translation: 1. Word-for-word translation. 2. Literal Translation. 3. Faithful Translation. 4. Communicative Translation. 5. Adaptation. 6. Free Translation.	Literary Texts Poems Texts with culture-specific problems Quotes Proverbs Module review exercises.	Translation from English into Arabic. Translation texts from Arabic into English to get more acquainted with the differences between SL and TL.	
Module 2: Literary Texts	1. Adaptation 2. Communicative Translation 3. Domestication 4. Foreignization Features of literary texts	Fiction Poetry Drama Module review exercises.	Translating texts from short stories and novels into English, applying translation strategies. Identifying cohesive devices and syntactic differences between SL and TL. Identifying and translating figures of speech.	Syntactic, Discourse and Cultural Problems.
Module 3: Economics Texts	Features of Economic Texts	Marketing Investment Banking Accounting and Audit Module review exercises.	Translating economics texts into English, paying attention to numbers and figures, false cognates and other translation problems. Translating texts that represent the basic economics genre.	Economics Terminology. Metaphors. False cognates.
Module 4: Scientific Texts	1. Borrowing. 2. Coinage. 3. Arabization. 4. Naturalization. Features of Scientific texts.	Chemistry Medicine Biology Epidemiology Module review exercises.	Translating scientific texts. Applying some of the strategies introduced in module 1 to scientific texts.	Word level equivalence. Above word level equivalence. Textual equivalence
Module 5: Media Texts	Features of Media Texts.	Conflicts/civil wars. Uprisings and revolutions. Elections and opposition. Natural disasters. Module review exercises.	Translation from English into Arabic. Translation of some extracts from Arabic into English. Wide range of drills on translating media texts. Summaries of texts into TL.	Syntactic problems. Culture-specific problems.
Module 6: Administrative Texts	Features of administrative texts.	Translating guidelines and regulations. Learning and teaching regulations. Glossaries from English into Arabic. Module review exercises.	Translating texts from Arabic into English. Translating texts from English into Arabic. Applying some translation strategies to translating administrative texts. Identifying and rectifying translation errors.	
Module 7: Legal Texts	Main features of legal texts. Types of legal texts.	Translating agreements and contracts. Security council: Terms and conditions. Peace Agreements. Glossaries English into Arabic. Module review exercises.	Translating legal texts into English. Translating legal texts into Arabic. Applying some of the translation strategies introduced in module 1. Identifying translation errors.	Syntactic problems. Culture-specific problems.

Foundation Methods of Translation

Before we discuss types of translation, a distinction should be first made between translation methods (or strategies) and translation procedures (or techniques). 'While translation methods relate to whole texts, translation procedures are used for sentences and the smaller units of language' (Newmark 1988a: 81). Methods of translation are classified into six types: word-for-word translation, literal translation, faithful translation, communicative translation, adaptation and free translation. These will be explained below with examples illustrating each type, followed by practice exercises for the learners. Other scholars have categorised translation strategies differently and various typologies exist (see Fawcett (1983), Ivir (1987), Larson (1984/1998), Vinay and Darbelnet (1958/1995) and Hervey and Higgins (2002)). This module will introduce the reader to these methods of translation, providing a variety of drills in order to contextualise and practise these methods.

LESSON 1: WORD-FOR-WORD TRANSLATION

This type of translation keeps the SL word order; words are translated out of context according to their most common meaning. Such kind of translation can be used as a preliminary translation step but it is not applied in real translation tasks. The following lines are from *The Secret Sharer* by Joseph Conrad with their translation into Arabic following the word-for-word method.

> On my right hand there were lines of fishing stakes resembling a mysterious system of half-submerged bamboo fences, incomprehensible in its division of the domain of tropical fishes.

Word-for-word translation will be:

> على يميني يد كانت خطوط الصيد حصص تشبه غموض نظام نصف مغمور لبامبو أسيجة غير مستوعب في تقسيمه لمجال الاستوائية الأسماك.

Such translation is meaningless to an Arab reader since neither its grammatical structure nor its semantics can help the reader make sense of what he or she reads. An acceptable translation would be:

> وكانت على يميني خطوط لأعمدة الصيد تشبه نظاما غامضا من سياج الخيزران نصف المغمورة غير المراعى في تقسيماتها لحركة الأسماك الاستوائية.

As we can see from the above example, word-for-word translation does not take context into consideration. It might be helpful as a first step in the translation but a great deal of editing and modifications have to be made in order to convey the message to the TL reader. The translator has to make sure that the translation follows the word order of the TL and that the choice of semantic equivalents is carried out accurately. Word-for-word translation can also be called *interlinear translation*.

1.1 Provide a word-for-word translation for the following excerpt, then provide an edited version.

They were new patients to me, all I had was the name, Olson. Please come down as soon as you can, my daughter is very sick.

When I arrived I was met by the mother, a big startled looking woman, very clean and apologetic who merely said, Is this the doctor? and let me in. In the back, she added. You must excuse us, doctor, we have her in the kitchen where it is warm. It is very damp here sometimes.

The child was fully dressed and sitting on her father's lap near the kitchen table. He tried to get up, but I motioned for him not to bother, took off my overcoat and started to look things over. I could see that they were all very nervous, eyeing me up and down distrustfully. As often, in such cases, they weren't telling me more than they had to, it was up to me to tell them; that's why they were spending three dollars on me.

The child was fairly eating me up with her cold, steady eyes, and no expression to her face whatever.

http://www.classicshorts.com/stories/force.html (accessed 17 October 2013)

Arabic translation

....

....

....

....

....

....

....

....

....

....

....

....

....

....

....

....

1.2 *Study the following Arabic word-for-word translation carefully and identify its problematic aspects.*

John had not much affection for his mother and sisters, and an antipathy to me. He bullied and punished me, not two or three times in the week, nor once or twice in the day, but continually; every nerve I had feared him and every morsel of flesh on my bones shrank when he comes near. There were moments when I was bewildered by the terror he inspired.

Jane Eyre, Emily Brontë

http://www.enotes.com/jane-eyre-text (accessed 12 March 2011)

جون كان لا كثيرا حب له أمه وأخواته وعداء لي. هو عذب وعاقب أنا ليس اثنان أو ثلاث مرات في الأسبوع، ليس مرة أو اثنتين في اليوم، لكن باستمرار، كل عصب أنا لي خاف هو وكل جزء من اللحم على لي عظم ارتجف عندما هو جاء قريب. كانت هناك لحظات عندما أنا كنت سيطرت بالرعب هو أوحى.

....

....

....

....

....

1.3 *Provide a translation that makes sense of the previous excerpt.*

....

....

....

....

....

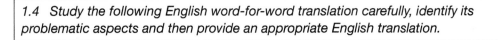

1.4 Study the following English word-for-word translation carefully, identify its problematic aspects and then provide an appropriate English translation.

حزن الصياد كثيرا لانه كان يذهب للصيد كل يوم دون ان يأتي بشيء. فقرر ان يترك المدينة ويهاجر الى مكان اخر لعل الحظ يبتسم له هذه المرة.

Sad the hunter much because was he go for hunting everyday without bringing anything. So decided he to leave city and migrate to place another may be luck smiles to him this time.

....

....

....

....

....

LESSON 2: LITERAL TRANSLATION

This type of translation preserves the grammatical structures of the SL where they are translated into their nearest TL equivalents. It takes place when the SL and TL share parallel structures. Words are translated out of context paying no attention to their connotative meanings. The following example illustrates this point.

To throw dust in the eyes.

يلقي التراب في العيون

The word 'dust' is translated literally as التراب while the equivalent expression in Arabic is يذرّ الرماد في العيون where 'dust' is translated into الرماد, ashes.

This choice could be justified by the cultural as well as ecological contexts that are different for both languages. If we take the English idiom *to throw dust in the eyes*, its associative meaning is based on the effect of dust once thrown in someone's eyes blurring their vision and impeding their ability to see. The same sense is expressed in Arabic by using the equivalent ashes rather than dust. Dust is, therefore, not expected to blur vision and hide reality in the Arabic context. Taking the English setting into consideration, you can rarely talk about deserts or dust storms. Another point has to do with religious rituals where some dust is thrown on the buried person in the grave.

2.1 Identify examples of literal translation in the following sentences.

1. I am afraid I lost all saved data. We are back to square one.

   أخشى أني فقدت كل البيانات المخزنة. عدنا للمربع الأول.

   ....

2. She decided to throw the baby with the bath water and close the shop forever because she lost few pounds.

   قرَّرتْ أن ترمي الطفل مع ماء الحمام وتغلق الدكان للأبد لأنها خسرَتْ بعض الجنيهات.

   ....

3. Hold your horses; we still have plenty of time.

   أمسك خيولك، لدينا الكثير من الوقت.

   ....

2.2   Provide correct translations for the sentences above.

....

....

....

....

....

2.3   Provide a literal translation for the following excerpt.

As doctors often do I took a trial shot at it as a point of departure. Has she had a sore throat?

Both parents answered me together, No . . . No, she says her throat don't hurt her. Does your throat hurt you? Added the mother to the child. But the little girl's expression didn't change nor did she move her eyes from my face. Have you looked? I tried to, said the mother, but I couldn't see.

....

....

....

....

2.4   Provide back translation for 2.3 and try to judge how accurate your literal translation was.

....

....

....

....

....

2.5 *Provide the correct translation for excerpt 2.3.*

....

....

....

....

....

....

LESSON 3: FAITHFUL TRANSLATION

This method maintains a balance between the literal meaning of the SL word and the TL syntactic structures. It sounds more reasonable as it takes the context into consideration, aiming at producing more precise meaning of the SL texts. Study the following quote by Shaw's *Back to Methuselah* (1921), Part 1, Act 1:

'You see things; and you say, "Why?" But I dream things that never were; and I say, "Why not?"'

It can be faithfully translated as:

أنت ترى الأشياء وتقول لماذا؟ ولكني أحلم بأشياء لم توجد أبدا وأقول لم لا؟

3.1 *Provide a faithful translation of the following quotes.*

1. For if the proper study of mankind is man, it is evidently more sensible to occupy yourself with the coherent, substantial and significant creatures of fiction than with the irrational and shadowy figures of real life.

W. Somerset Maugham (1874–1965), British novelist and playwright

http://en.proverbia.net/citastema.asp?tematica=470 (accessed 12 March 2011)

....
....
....
....
....

2. Fiction is like a spider's web, attached ever so lightly perhaps, but still attached to life at all four corners. Often the attachment is scarcely perceptible.

Virginia Woolf (1882–1941), British novelist and essayist

http://en.proverbia.net/citastema.asp?tematica=470&page=2 (accessed 12 March 2011)

....

....

....

....

....

3.2 Read the Arabic translation below of the following poem and comment on the strategy used for translation.

Requiem
By Robert Louis Stevenson

Under the wide and starry sky,
Dig the grave and let me lie.
Glad did I live and gladly die,
And I laid me down with a will.

This be the verse you grave for me:
Here he lies where he longed to be;
Home is the sailor, home from the sea,
And the hunter home from the hill.

http://www.poetry-archive.com/s/requiem.html (accessed 12 March 2011)

Arabic translation

تحت سماء رحبة مرصعة بالنجوم
لتحفرْ قبري وتدعني أستلقي
سعيدا عشت وسعيدا أموت
ومعي أرقدت وصية
فلترْثيني بهذه الأبيات
عاد البحّار لبيته، عاد من البحر
والصياد من التلال

....

....

....

....

....

3.3   *Translate the following stanzas and explain the method(s) you have used.*

To a Skylark
By Percy Bysshe Shelley

What objects are the fountains
Of thy happy strain?
What fields, or waves, or mountains?
What shapes of sky or plain?
What love of thine own kind? what ignorance of pain?
With thy clear keen joyance
Languor cannot be:
Shadow of annoyance
Never came near thee:
Thou lovest, but ne'er knew love's sad satiety.
Waking or asleep,
Thou of death must deem
Things more true and deep
Than we mortals dream,
Or how could thy notes flow in such a crystal stream?

http://www.netpoets.com/classic/poems/057025.htm (accessed 12 March 2011)

....
....
....
....
....
....
....
....
....
....
....
....
....
....

LESSON 4: COMMUNICATIVE TRANSLATION

This type of translation attempts to render the exact contextual meaning of the original text in such a way that both content and language are readily acceptable and comprehensible to the reader. It is particularly suitable when translating conventional formulae or proverbs and it involves some levels of cultural approximation. Communicative translation aspires to create the same effect created by the SL text on the TL reader. Though it is not as accurate as semantic translation which sticks to the original text, it communicates the meaning at the expense of accuracy. However, it is preferred by many translators because it resorts to concepts that are more familiar to the TL reader on cultural and social levels. It is usually used for culturally specific idioms, proverbs or clichés where the translator replaces a SL word or concept with one that already exists in the TL. Communicative translation concentrates on the message and the main force of the text, tends to be simple, clear and brief, and is always written in a natural and resourceful style (Newmark (1988: 48). For some linguists, communicative translation 'is produced, when, in a given situation, the ST uses a SL expression standard for that situation, and the TT uses a TL expression standard for an equivalent target culture situation' (Dickins et al. 2005: 17). Study the following examples:

Charity begins at home.

الأقربون أولى بالمعروف.

Diamonds cut diamonds.

لا يفل الحديد إلا الحديد.

Notice here that 'diamonds' is rendered by حديد which is equivalent to *iron* in English. Literal translation would not convey the message here. In Arabic 'diamond' has positive associations related to beauty and noble characteristics while iron is associated with strength and physical power. Prophet Mohammad said:

"النَّاسُ مَعَادِنُ كَمَعَادِنِ الذَّهَبِ وَالْفِضَّةِ, خِيَارُهُمْ فِي الْجَاهِلِيَّةِ خِيَارُهُمْ فِي الإِسْلامِ إِذَا فَقِهُوا"

This translates as follows: 'People are like metals such as gold and silver. The good ones before Islam are also good when converted as long as they learn about Islam.' Diamond, then, is used in Arabic to refer to how good or bad a person is.

Iron is cut by iron

لا يفل الحديد إلا الحديد

Road signs, greetings and compliments are best rendered by communicative translation as shown in the following examples.

Dead end, no exit: طريق غير نافذ
Detour: تحويلة
Bus, load/unload: موقف باص\تحميل\تنزيل

As for everyday greetings, communicative translation is preferred, especially for colloquial phrases. For example, 'long time no see' is best rendered by زمان هالقمر ما با ن. Note also the differences in the following dialogue:

Kim: Hi, Ann. What's happening?
Ann: Not much. You?

The communicative translation will be:

كيم: مرحبا آن, ما أخبارك؟
آن: لا جديد, ماذا عنك؟

Here the usual formula used for everyday communication was used rather than the literal translation for 'not much'.

4.1 Translate the following English proverbs using communicative translation.

1. A burnt child dreads the fire.

   ....

2. A cat has nine lives.

   ....

3. Don't count your chickens before they're hatched

   ....

4. Let bygones be bygones.

   ....

5. Marriage is a lottery.

   ....

4.2 *Translate the following dialogue using communicative translation.*

Brother: Are you sure you want to tell him?

Sister: We should, he has the right to know?

Brother: Don't forget, he has serious heart issues when he gets exposed to surprises?

Sister: I know, I know. Besides, he knew all of this already, before the accident happened.

Brother: Ok, he might have damaged half of his brain nerves and lost ¾ of his memory, but …

Sister: He has the right to know!

Brother: Fine, but if anything goes wrong, it is your fault. Got it?

http://www.bukisa.com/articles/358889_example-of-use-of-dialogue-in-drama (accessed 12 June 2011)

....

....

....

....

....

....

....

 4.3 *Translate the following Arabic proverbs into English using communicative translation.*

1- عصفور في اليد ولا عشرة على الشجرة.

....

2- في العجلة الندامة .

....

3- غاب القط العب يا فار.

....

4- الطيور على اشكالها تقع.

....

5- رب ضارة نافعة.

....

LESSON 5: ADAPTATION

This strategy is considered as the freest form of translation, and it is not usually differentiated from the following types (free translation). Adaptation is used mainly for plays (comedies) and poetry; the themes, characters and plots are usually preserved, the SL culture is converted to the TL culture and the text is rewritten. This strategy will be dealt with in detail in the drama section. The following excerpt from Shaw's *Pygmalion* (1912) is translated into Lebanese Arabic where names of places are replaced by Lebanese villages.

> THE NOTE TAKER:
> And how are all your people down at Selsey?
>
> THE BYSTANDER:
> [Suspiciously] Who told you my people come from Selsey?
>
> وكيف أهلك في سرغيتا ؟
>
> وشو عرّفك إني من سرغيتا؟

Selsey is translated as سرغيتا, a village in Lebanon. This choice might be justified by the translator's attempt to adapt the play to the Lebanese setting; thus choosing a village in the Lebanese countryside as well as a Lebanese dialect in the translation.

5.1 *Translate the following sentences, adapting them to the English culture.*

1- اشترت مريم فستانا بخمسين دينار.

....

2- يا اخي ، اقبل دعوتك للعشاء ولو كان صحن سلطة.

....

3- عيون هذا الطفل جميلة كعيون البقر.

....

5.2 *Translate the following excerpt from Act 1 of Shaw's* Arms and the Man, *adapting it to the culture of an Arab country you are familiar with.*

RAINA [laughing and sitting down again] Yes, I was only a prosaic little coward. Oh, to think that it was all true – that Sergius is just as splendid and noble as he looks – that the world is really a glorious world for women who can see its glory and men who can act its romance! What happiness! What unspeakable fulfillment! Ah! [She throws herself on her knees beside her mother and flings her arms passionately round her. They are interrupted by the entry of Louka, a handsome, proud girl in a pretty Bulgarian peasant's dress with double apron, so defiant that her servility to Raina is almost insolent. She is afraid of Catherine, but even with her goes as far as she dares. She is just now excited like the others; but she has no sympathy for Raina's raptures and looks contemptuously at the ecstasies of the two before she addresses them.]

http://www.archive.org/stream/armsthemanantiro00shawuoft/armsthemanantiro00shaw uoft_djvu.txt (accessed 1 June 2011)

....

....

....

....

....

....

....

....

....

....

....

....

....

....

You can choose Arabic names for people and places, clothes and food. Your translation should reflect the culture you are translating into.

5.3   Translate the following sentences, adapting them to the English culture.

1. الله يعطيك العافية. ....

2. صبر عليه صبر الجمال. ....

3. ارا ك غدا ان شاء الله. ....

4. عظم الله اجركم. ....

5. السلام عليكم. ....

5.4   Translate the following proverbs from English adapting them to the Arabic culture.

1. The proof of the pudding is in the eating.

    ....

2. Love me, love my dog.

    ....

3. A Jack of all trades is a master of none.

    ....

4. Haste is waste.

    ....

5. Still waters run deep.

    ....

LESSON 6: FREE TRANSLATION

This strategy preserves the meaning of the original but uses natural forms of the TL, including normal word order and syntax, so that the translation can be naturally understood. It preserves the content at the expense of the form, and it provides a longer paraphrase of the original. It is a form of idiomatic translation that favours colloquialisms and idioms which do not exist in the SL. The following is a part of *Cinderella* and its translation into Arabic:

Cinderella had a wonderful time at the ball until she heard the first stroke of midnight! She remembered what the fairy had said, and without a word of goodbye she slipped from the Prince's arms and ran down the steps. As she ran she lost one of her slippers, but not for a moment did she dream of stopping to pick it up! If the last stroke of midnight were to sound ... oh ... what a disaster that would be! Out she fled and vanished into the night.

أمضت سندريلا وقتا في غاية المتعة في حفلة الرقص حتى سمعت دقات الساعة تعلن حلول منتصف الليل فتذكرت ما قالته الجنية فانسلت من غير بخاطركم ولا مع السلامة بخلسة من بين يدي الأمير ونزلت الدرج بسرعة. وبينما كانت تركض سقطت منها إحدى فردتي الحذاء لكنها لم تتوقف ولم تحدث نفسها حتى بالتوقف لأنها إن فعلت ذلك فيا ويلها ويا سواد ليلها فركضت مسرعة واختفت في الظلام.

Notice that we have longer expressions in the TL. For example, 'a wonderful time' is translated into في غاية المتعة instead of ممتعا. Colloquial expressions are also used as illustrated in the following examples.

Without a word of goodbye: من غير بخاطركم ولا مع السلامة

What a disaster would that be! يا ويلها ويا سواد ليلها

6.1 Identify the features of free translation.

....

....

....

....

6.2   Provide a free translation of the following text.

Now two women *who were* harlots came to the king, and stood before him. And one woman said, 'O my lord, this woman and I dwell in the same house; and I gave birth while she *was* in the house. Then it happened, the third day after I had given birth, that this woman also gave birth. And we *were* together; no one *was* with us in the house, except the two of us in the house. And this woman's son died in the night, because she lay on him. So she arose in the middle of the night and took my son from my side, while your maidservant slept, and laid him in her bosom, and laid her dead child in my bosom. And when I rose in the morning to nurse my son, there he was, dead. But when I had examined him in the morning, indeed, he was not my son whom I had borne.'

http://www.biblegateway.com/passage/?search=1+Kings+3%3A16-28&version=NKJV
(accessed 25 March 2011)

....

....

....

....

....

....

....

....

....

....

....

....

....

....

Other specific translation strategies that are followed in translating scientific and economic texts will be discussed in detail in the modules on economic and scientific translation.

MODULE REVIEW EXERCISES

1. Illustrate with examples the differences between word–for–word and literal translation.

....

....

....

....

....

2. Provide a faithful translation for the following excerpt.

THE POMEGRANATE and Apple-Tree disputed as to which was the most beautiful. When their strife was at its height, a Bramble from the neighbouring hedge lifted up its voice, and said in a boastful tone: 'Pray, my dear friends, in my presence at least cease from such vain disputing.'

....

....

....

....

....

3. Apply communicative translation to one of your chosen literary genres. Share your translation with a colleague and work together on evaluating each other's translation, then present your findings to the class.

....

....

....

....

....

....

20

....
....
....
....
....
....

---

4. *Translate the following dialogue following adaptation strategy.*

Open on a living room in Africa. Enter the INDIAN BUTLER
INDIAN BUTLER: Curry? Senor, Curry?
Enter TOLSTOY and ANNA
ANNA Hello, our Indian Butler, I wonder what you might be doing?
TOLSTOY: Yes, I wonder.
INDIAN BUTLER: I am selling Curry.
TOLSTOY and BULTER begin Curry Song
TOLSTOY: I enjoy fine dining!
BUTLER: I enjoy refining!
TOLSTOY: Cracking plants are the life for me!
BUTLER: And the monkey ...
TOLSTOY: Yes the monkey!

http://drama.eserver.org/plays/contemporary/tolstoy-in-the-GPAAS.txt (accessed
25 October 2013)

....
....
....
....
....
....
....
....
....
....
....
....

⟳ | 5. *Provide a free translation of the following quotes.*

1. In three words I can sum up everything I've learned about life: it goes on. Robert Frost.

   ....

2. Throughout life people will make you mad, disrespect you and treat you bad. Let God deal with the things they do, cause hate in your heart will consume you too. Will Smith.

   ....

   ....

   ....

3. Never be bullied into silence. Never allow yourself to be made a victim. Accept no one's definition of your life; define yourself. Harvey Fierstein.

   ....

   ....

   ....

⟳ | 6. *Provide a communicative translation of the following nursery rhyme.*

Hush, little baby, don't say a word,
Mama's going to buy you
a mockingbird.
And if that mockingbird won't sing,
Mama's going to buy you
a diamond ring.

www.nurseryrhymes.com (accessed 25 October 2013)

....

....

....

....

....

Literary Texts

Literary translation, as other types of translations, makes the reader aware of the existence of literary works of other cultures. It helps him or her read such works and appreciate them, thus fostering cultural dialogue. Indeed, literary works of various cultures have been translated into other cultures all over the world. One can talk about a universal literary canon that was established via literary translation. Literary figures in almost all cultures are universally acknowledged, thanks to the role of translation in promoting such a work. Who does not know about Shakespeare's *Romeo and Juliet* or *One Thousand and One Nights*?

Translating literary texts is not an easy task. It is more demanding than other types of translation since it deals with two cultures, a source culture and a target one. The translator has the duty of a social mediator between both cultures since it is necessary to decide on how to translate concepts represented in the SL and TL using different ideas and images and how to translate idiomatic expressions that may carry extra meaning in the translated literary genre. Furthermore, sometimes translated work is published and this makes the job more demanding since the demands of the publisher, readers and writers have to be met.

> A translated text, whether prose or poetry, fiction or nonfiction, is judged acceptable by most publishers, reviewers and readers when it reads fluently, when the absence of any linguistics or stylistic peculiarities makes it seem transparent, giving the appearance that it reflects the foreign writer's personality or intention or the essential meaning of the foreign text. (Venuti 2008: 1)

The basic literary genres that will be dealt with in this module are fiction, drama and poetry. Each section will tackle the distinctive features of the genre, problems encountered in translation and strategies to deal with these problems.

LESSON 7: FICTION

The word 'fiction' is used in literature to refer to a literary genre that is characterised by narration. It is usually prose written in the form of a novel, a short story or a novella and this section will discuss these types of fiction. You can refer to any introductory book on literary genres for other types. As a literary genre, fiction has been sub-classified into themes such as mystery, historical, romance, fantasy, western, science fiction, action/adventure, humour, medical, tragedy, thriller, horror, in addition to other types.

Translating fiction is challenging in general since it relies heavily on narration (see next section). Each sub-genre of fiction has its linguistic characteristics. Furthermore, the translator has to make a decision regarding being source-language-oriented or target-language-oriented. Adapting, managing or monitoring are other issues that the translator of fiction is faced with while translating different genres of fiction.

When translating from English into Arabic, the translator's job is even more demanding since these languages belong to two different language families. Arabic is a Semitic language while English is Indo-European. Both languages have different syntactic, phonological and lexical systems, in addition to the complicated cultural differences.

This section will present some exercises to help you practise strategies for translating some extracts from novels and short stories from English into Arabic.

7.1 Read the following SL and TL texts then find examples of adaptation strategies and comment on them.

He was an old man who fished alone in a skiff in the Gulf Stream and he had gone eighty-four days now without taking a fish. In the first forty days a boy had been with him. But after forty days without a fish the boy's parents had told him that the old man was now definitely and finally salao [to be unlucky in fishing], which is the worst form of unlucky, and the boy had gone at their orders in another boat which caught three good fish the first week. It made the boy sad to see the old man come in each day with his skiff empty.

The Old Man and the Sea, Ernest Hemingway

كان يا ما كان في قديم الزمان, كان هناك رجل اعتاد الصيد لوحده في مركب شراعي صغير في البحر. وقد مضى عليه أربعة وثمانون يوما دون أن يصطاد ولو سمكة واحدة.

وقد صحبه فتى في الأيام الأربعين الأولى ولكن بعد ذلك طلب والدا الفتى منه أن يذهب في قارب آخر لأن الرجل حظه قليل. أطاع الفتى أمر والديه وذهب في قارب آخر واصطاد ثلاث سمكات في الأسبوع الأول. حزن الفتى لرؤية الرجل العجوز يعود خالي الوفاض كل يوم.

7.2 Translate the following excerpt from Nineteen Eighty-four *by George Orwell, following the translation method you find most appropriate. Explain why you have opted for a particular method.*

It was a peculiarly beautiful book. Its smooth creamy paper, a little yellowed by age, was of a kind that had not been manufactured for at least forty years past. He could guess, however, that the book was much older than that. He had seen it lying in the window of a frowsy little junk-shop in a slummy quarter of the town (just what quarter he did not now remember) and had been stricken immediately by an overwhelming desire to possess it. Party members were supposed not to go into ordinary shops ('dealing on the free market', it was called), but the rule was not strictly kept, because there were various things, such as shoelaces and razor blades, which it was impossible to get hold of in any other way.

....

....

....

....

....

....

....

....

....

7.3 Follow communicative translation to translate the following lines from The Lottery, *a short story by Shirley Jackson.*

The morning of June 27th was clear and sunny, with the fresh warmth of a full-summer day; the flowers were blossoming profusely and the grass was richly green. The people of the village began to gather in the square, between the post office and the bank, around ten o'clock; in some towns there were so many people that the lottery took two days and had to be started on June 2th. But in this village, where there were only about three hundred people, the whole lottery took less than two hours, so it could begin at ten o'clock in the morning and still be through in time to allow the villagers to get home for noon dinner.

....

....

....

....

....

....

....

....

LESSON 8: NARRATIVE TEXTS: DISCOURSE PROBLEMS

Narration is the most distinctive feature of fiction. It forms the plot of the story or the novel which has a specific setting and a point of view that is the voice of the narrator. The reader is taken on a journey by the narrator to follow a conflict that builds up to reach a climax and is usually followed by a resolution. The translator's awareness of elements of fiction and narrative techniques facilitates the translation process. Narrative is defined as:

> one method of recapitulating past experience by matching a verbal sequence of clauses to the sequence of events which (it is inferred) actually occurred ... Within this conception of narrative, we can define a *minimal narrative* as a sequence of two clauses which are temporally ordered: that is, a change in their order will result in a change in the temporal sequence of the original semantic interpretation. (Labov (1972: 360)

Narrative as a genre has a fibula that consists of chronologically related events; a narrative text has two types of spokesmen where one does not play a role in the fibula whereas the other one does (Bal 1985: 5). Narrative texts contain three layers: the text, the story and the fibula, and they deal with a series of connected events caused or experienced by the actors (ibid.). More details on prose and narration can be found in other books (for example, Amigoni 2000).

Discourse problems are related to the aspects of cohesion and coherence in Arabic and English. Arabic, for example, relies heavily on conjunction as a cohesive device while English uses more subordination. It is usual to have run-on sentences in Arabic since punctuation is not traditionally utilised as a cohesive device. While English uses subordinates and general words as lexical cohesive devices, Arabic favours repetition of the same lexical item (Dickins 2002 and 2009).

According to a comprehensive taxonomy, cohesive devices in English can be classified as reference, substitution, ellipsis, conjunction and lexical cohesion. Each device is dealt with inclusively, and is applied to samples of narrative texts (Halliday and Hasan 1976). Reference, conjunction and lexical cohesion are expected to be more frequent than substitution and ellipsis, which might be more frequent in drama.

8.1 *Read and analyse the following Arabic and English narrative texts. Identify the five cohesive devices, taking into consideration the distinctive characteristics of fiction which is based on narrative.*

The Ant and the Dove

An Ant went to the bank of a river to quench its thirst, and being carried away by the rush of the stream, was on the point of drowning. A Dove sitting on a tree overhanging the water plucked a leaf and let it fall into the stream close to her. The Ant climbed onto it and floated in safety to the bank. Shortly afterwards a bird catcher came and stood under the tree, and laid his lime-twigs for the Dove, which sat in the branches. The Ant, perceiving his design, stung him in the foot. In pain the bird catcher threw down the twigs, and the noise made the Dove take wing.

http://www.aesopfables.com/cgi/aesop1.cgi?sel&TheAntandtheDove&&antdove.ram
(accessed 28 March 2011)

....

....

....

....

....

....

....

....

....

في أحد الأيام وفي قرية صغيرة ريفية جميلة كان يوجد راعٍ يأخذ حيوانات القرية إلى المراعي المجاورة في الصباح الباكر ويعيدها في المساء.

وفي ذات يوم جميل خطر في بال هذا الراعي فكرة إخافة أهل قريته فصعد على مرتفع يطل على قريته وبدأ يصيح وينادي أكلتني الذئاب والوحوش أنا وجميع الحيوانات أسرعوا.

فما أن سمع أهل القرية هذا حتى تركوا أعمالهم جميعها وحملوا أسلحتهم بأيديهم وذهبوا إليه ولما وصلوا إلى عنده بدأ الراعي يضحك ويهزأ منهم فعاد أهل القرية إلى قريتهم.

وبعد عدة أيام كرر الراعي هذه القصة مع أهل القرية وظل يكررها يوما بعد يوم. وفي صباح أحد الأيام وقبل أن يكررها كعادته التّمّت وتجمعت الوحوش والذئاب الجائعة حوله وحول حيوانات أهل القرية فبدأ يصيح بأعلى صوته: ((أكلتني الذئاب والوحوش أنا وجميع الحيوانات أسرعوا)) إنني لا اكذب عليكم هذه المرة. سمع أهل القرية صياح الراعي ولكنهم لم يكترثوا له.

غابت الشمس وحان موعد عودة الراعي و الحيوانات إلى القرية وحل الظلام ولم يعد الراعي حتى الآن فاجتمع أهل القرية وتوجهوا إلى مكان الراعي فلم يشاهدوا سوى ملابس الراعي الممزقة وبعض العظام. فعادوا إلى قريتهم حزينين. وأصبحوا يطلقون عليه وهو ميت ** الراعي الكذاب**.

http://www.qassimy.com/st1/lesson-677-1.html (accessed 28 March 2011)

....

....

....

....

....

....

....

....

....

....

8.2 *Read the following extracts and identify the cohesive devices used. Compare and contrast the cohesive devices in the SL and TL.*

When I came home to dinner my uncle had not yet been home. Still it was early. I sat staring at the clock for some time and, when its ticking began to irritate me, I left the room. I mounted the staircase and gained the upper part of the house. The high, cold, empty, gloomy rooms liberated me and I went from room to room singing. From the front window I saw my companions playing below in the street. Their cries reached me weakened and indistinct and, leaning my forehead against the cool glass, I looked over at the dark house where she lived.

Araby, James Joyce

http://www.uk.sagepub.com/upm-data/9680_011352.pdf (accessed 28 March 2011)

Arabic translation

عندما عدت لتناول العشاء لم يكن عمي قد عاد إلى البيت بعد، فقد كان الوقت ما يزال مبكرا على عودته، فجلست أنظر إلى ساعة الحائط لبعض الوقت وعندما بدأ صوت دقاتها يزعجني غادرت الغرفة وصعدت الدرج إلى الجزء الأعلى من البيت، وقد حررتني الغرف الباردة والفارغة والداكنة فجعلت أتحرك من غرفة لأخرى وأنا أغني. ثم شاهدت من الشباك الأمامي رفقائي يلعبون في الشارع حيث وصل صراخهم إلي خافتا مشوشا فطأطأت رأسي على الزجاج البارد ونظرت إلى البيت المظلم حيث كانت تعيش.

....

....

....

....

....

....

....

 8.3 *Translate the following extract from* Hard Times *by Charles Dickens.*

'Fact, fact, fact!' said the gentleman. And 'Fact, fact, fact!' repeated Thomas Gradgrind. 'You are to be in all things regulated and governed,' said the gentleman, 'by fact. We hope to have, before long, a board of fact, composed of commissioners of fact, who will force the people to be a people of fact, and of nothing but fact. You must discard the word Fancy altogether. You have nothing to do with it. You are not to have, in any object of use or ornament, what would be a contradiction in fact. You don't walk upon flowers in fact; you cannot be allowed to walk upon flowers in carpets. You don't find that foreign birds and butterflies come and perch upon your crockery; you cannot be permitted to paint foreign birds and butterflies upon your crockery. You never meet with quadrupeds going up and down walls; you must not have quadrupeds represented upon walls. You must use,' said the gentleman, 'for all these purposes, combinations and modifications (in primary colours) of mathematical figures which are susceptible of proof and demonstration. This is the new discovery. This is fact. This is taste.'

Glossary

Commissioners	مفوضون	**Modifications**	تعديلات
A board	مجلس	**Susceptible**	قابل ل
Contradiction	تناقض	**Discovery**	اكتشاف
Combinations	مزج		

....

....

....

....

....

....

....

....

....

LESSON 9: NARRATIVE TEXTS: SYNTACTIC PROBLEMS

Syntax is another problematic area for translators working with Arabic and English texts. Though both languages share some syntactic universals, many differences still challenge the translator. While English is usually considered an SVO (Subject-Verb-Object) language, Arabic is basically a VSO language since SVO structures are less frequent. A translator from English into Arabic must take this difference into consideration. English makes use of auxiliary verbs in questions and negation. Such use is not frequent in Arabic. Therefore, auxiliary verbs are not always translated into Arabic.

Tense also constitutes a challenge for translators who are not fully aware of the Arabic tense. Arabic tense is classified into past, present and future. It depends on inflections of both the verb and the subject to convey the meaning associated with the use of a certain tense. One form of the verb is used to convey different categories of past or present. Adverbs are used sometimes to indicate different tenses. Study the following English sentences:

Mark went to school.

Mark has gone to school.

Both sentences are rendered by:

When I had finished my work, I went for a walk.   ذهب مارك إلى المدرسة.

عندما أنهيت عملي خرجت في نزهة.

I finished my work yesterday.

أنهيت عملي أمس.

Notice that both 'finished' and 'had finished' are translated as أنهيت. The simple past tense might be less problematic than the perfect whose equivalent is not easily found in Arabic. Instead, Arabic usually uses adverbs to indicate the perfective aspect. Consider the following examples:

They have just arrived from the airport.

وصلوا من المطار توا أو حالا.

They arrived from the airport yesterday.

وصلوا من المطار أمس.

As can be seen, an adverb had to be added to convey the perfect aspect in Arabic. For the present perfect you need to add adverbs such as في التو, توا, حالا, على الفور, or لتوهم.

Furthermore, the construction كان+ قد with its derivatives is used to convey the past perfect as shown in the following example:

> She felt sad about losing her watch because she had had it for twenty years.
>
> شعرت بالحزن لأنها أضاعت ساعتها لأنها كانت قد احتفظت بها عشرين عاما.

The progressive aspect is not rendered by auxiliary verbs in Arabic though some varieties of colloquial Arabic do have equivalents for auxiliaries used with the progressive aspect. Standard Arabic, however, depends on the use of adverbs to convey the progressive aspect. It combines كان and its derivatives with the past progressive as illustrated in the following examples:

> My sister is waiting for me at the park.
>
> أختي تنتظرني في المنتزه.
>
> Alice was beginning to get very tired of sitting by her sister on the bank, and of having nothing to do.
>
> كانت أليس قد بدأت تتعب من الجلوس بجانب أختها على ضفة النهر ومن عدم وجود شيء لتفعله.

 9.1 *Translate the following from* Alice's Adventures in Wonderland *by Lewis Carroll, marking the syntactic differences between Arabic and English.*

Alice was beginning to get very tired of sitting by her sister on the bank, and of having nothing to do: once or twice she had peeped into the book her sister was reading, but it had no pictures or conversations in it, 'and what is the use of a book,' thought Alice 'without pictures or conversation?'

So she was considering in her own mind (as well as she could, for the hot day made her feel very sleepy and stupid) whether the pleasure of making a daisy-chain would be worth the trouble of getting up and picking the daisies, when suddenly a White Rabbit with pink eyes ran close by her.

There was nothing so VERY remarkable in that; nor did Alice think it so VERY much out of the way to hear the Rabbit say to itself, 'Oh dear! Oh dear! I shall be late!' (When she thought it over afterwards, it occurred to her that she ought to have wondered at this, but at the time it all seemed quite natural.)

....

....

....

....

....

....

....

....

....

....

....

....

9.2   Translate the following excerpt from The Haunted House *by Charles Dickens and identify five different tenses in the SL and TL.*

Under none of the accredited ghostly circumstances, and environed by none of the conventional ghostly surroundings, did I first make acquaintance with the house which is the subject of this Christmas piece. I saw it in the daylight, with the sun upon it. There was no wind, no rain, no lightning, no thunder, and no awful or unwanted circumstance, of any kind, to heighten its effect. More than that: I had come to it direct from a railway station: it was not more than a mile distant from the railway station; and, as I stood outside the house, looking back upon the way I had come, I could see the goods train running smoothly along the embankment in the valley. I will not say that everything was utterly commonplace, because I doubt if anything can be that, except to utterly commonplace people – and there my vanity steps in; but, I will take it on myself to say that anybody might see the house as I saw it, any fine autumn morning.

http://www.classichorrorstories.com/texts/hauntedh.txt (accessed 11 April 2011)

Glossary

Circumstances	ظروف	**Vanity**	تكبر
Make acquaintance with	يتعرف إلى	**Commonplace**	مألوف
Embankment	سكة القطار		

....

....

....

....

....

....

....

....

....

....

....

....

....

....

9.3 *Translate the following Arabic text into English and identify the problematic tenses.*

ذهبت نملة صغيرة إلى جدول ماء لتشرب وتستريح، بعد أن تعبت كثيراً في جمع قوتها. فزلّت قدمها وسقطت في الماء، ولم يمكنها الخروج منه، لأنّها لا تعرف السباحة وكادت تغرق.

وكانت حمامة بيضاء جميلة واقفة على حجر في الماء، ورأت ما حصل للنملة. فرقّ لها قلبها وسعت في خلاصها، فطارت إلى البرّ ورجعت، وفي منقارها عود من الحشيش، مدّته على الماء إلى البرّ. فتعلّقت به النملة وخرجت من الماء بسلام.

http://darsulmahad.blogspot.com/2011/08/blog-post_7180.html (accessed 28 July 2013)

....

....

....

....

....

....

....

LESSON 10: CULTURAL PROBLEMS, DOMESTICATION AND FOREIGNISATION

Translation is not simply a matter of translating words. When you translate, you are working with language and culture. Language is one of the many social activities through which the culture of its speakers is manifested. As a translator, you need to understand the culture of the audience you are communicating with. You are standing as a mediator between the SL and TL. If the SL is your mother tongue, then half of the problem is solved. All that you need to do is to understand the cultural background of the target reader/audience so as to be able to convey the SL message to them. You need to develop a strategy that can help you tackle culture-bound idioms for instance. Cultural problems in translation are also related to the sociolinguistic aspects of language such as politeness and terms of address, as well as aspects related to discourse. Such aspects involve speech acts, maxims of speech, implicature, inference and presupposition. The translator should be aware of how these concepts are manifested in each culture.

There are various ways to deal with these aspects of cultures as they occur in texts. You can make use of the following steps for translating culturally bound words (Graedler 2000: 3):

- Making up a new word.
- Explaining the meaning of the SL expression in lieu of translating it.
- Preserving the SL term intact.
- Opting for a word in the TL which seems similar to or has the same 'relevance' as the SL term.

The following strategies are suggested to deal with culturally bound words (Harvey 2000: 2–6):

- Functional Equivalence: where a referent in the TL culture whose function is similar to that of the SL referent is used.
- Formal Equivalence, 'linguistic equivalence' or 'word-for-word' translation.
- Transcription or 'borrowing' (i.e. reproducing or, where necessary, transliterating the original term): it stands at the far end of SL-oriented strategies.
- Descriptive or self-explanatory translation: using generic terms to convey the meaning.

As we see, different authors give different names to strategies for dealing with these words. In general, Newmark (1988a: 96) provides two methods to deal with cultural problems in translation, namely, transference and componential analysis. He states that transference gives 'local colour', keeping cultural names and concepts, and this includes transliteration. Newmark stresses the importance of the translation process in communication suggesting componential analysis, which he describes as being 'the most accurate translation procedure, which excludes the culture and highlights the message' (Newmark 1988a: 96). It involves 'comparing an SL word with a TL word which has a similar meaning but is not an obvious one-to-one equivalent, by demonstrating first their common and then their differing sense components' (Newmark 1988b: 114).

10.1 *Translate the following text and identify the steps and strategies you followed.*

ALL around everything was still as far as the ear could reach. The mist of his feelings shifted between us, as if disturbed by his struggles, and in the rifts of the immaterial veil he would appear to my staring eyes distinct of form and pregnant with vague appeal like a symbolic figure in a picture. The chill air of the night seemed to lie on my limbs as heavy as a slab of marble.

'I see,' I murmured, more to prove to myself that I could break my state of numbness than for any other reason.

'The Avondale picked us up just before sunset,' he remarked, moodily. 'Steamed right straight for us. We had only to sit and wait.'

Lord Jim, Joseph Conrad, Chapter 12

 Glossary

Disturbed	مضطرب	Distinct	مميّز
Immaterial	روحي	Numbness	خدر
Symbolic	رمزي		

....

....

....

....

....

....

....

....

....

10.2   Translate the following text keeping cultural names and concepts and using transliteration where needed.

Once, when Roger was a young boy, his father took him to an open day at Nellis AFB, out in the California desert. Sunlight glared brilliantly from the polished silver plate flanks of the big bombers, sitting in their concrete-lined dispersal bays behind barriers and blinking radiation monitors. The brightly coloured streamers flying from their pitot tubes lent them a strange, almost festive appearance. But they were sleeping nightmares: once awakened, nobody – except the flight crew – could come within a mile of the nuclear-powered bombers and live.

AFB = Air Force Base

Pitot tube = a pressure instrument used to measure fluid flow velocity

http://www.infinityplus.co.uk/stories/colderwar.htm (accessed 19 April 2011)

....

....

....

....

....

....

....

....

....

....

There are other strategies that can be utilised to bridge cultural gaps in translation. These include domestication and foreignisation (Venuti 1995: 49). Domestication aims at making the translated text closer to the TL culture where 'the foreign text is imprinted with values specific to the target-language culture' (Venuti 1995: 49). Foreignisation, on the other hand, preserves the values of the ST in the sense that it 'resists dominant target-language cultural values so as to signify the linguistic and cultural difference of the foreign text' (ibid.). Foreignisation is seen as an ethical issue because in English it 'can be a form of resistance against ethnocentrism and racism, cultural narcissism and imperialism, in the interests of democratic geopolitical relations' (ibid. p. 20).

Those who support domestication argue that it helps the reader understand the text easily. Others suggest that domestication blurs acculturation and discourage critical thought that challenges the TL.

The following examples illustrate the distinction between domestication and foreignisation.

English	Domesticated Arabic Translation	Foreignised Arabic Translation
I will see you Friday noon in the <u>bar.</u>	أراك ظهر الجمعة في <u>المقهى.</u>	أراك ظهر الجمعة في <u>الحانة.</u>
Thousands <u>were killed</u> in the raid.	<u>استشهد</u> آلاف في الغارة.	<u>قتل</u> آلاف في الغارة.
Their story reminds you of <u>Romeo and Juliet.</u>	تذكرك قصتهم <u>بقيس وليلى</u> .	تذكرك قصتهم <u>برومبو وجولييت.</u>

10.3 *Translate the following excerpt into Arabic following the strategies of domestication and foreignisation. Then cite examples for both strategies.*

Once upon a time, there was a little girl who lived in a village near the forest. Whenever she went out, the little girl wore a red riding cloak, so everyone in the village called her Little Red Riding Hood.

One morning, Little Red Riding Hood asked her mother if she could go to visit her grandmother as it had been awhile since they'd seen each other.

'That's a good idea,' her mother said. So they packed a nice basket for Little Red Riding Hood to take to her grandmother.

http://www.dltk-teach.com/rhymes/littlered/1.htm (accessed 19 April 2011)

Foreignisation

....

....

....

....

....

Domestication

....

....

....

....

....

....

....

....

....

....

LESSON 11: DRAMA

Drama as a literary genre differs from fiction. In essence, it is written to be performed on stage. Therefore, dialogue plays a considerable role in drama. Moreover, drama is not only a literary piece; it is a cultural one. The translator deals with both linguistic and meta-linguistic elements that include body language and gesture. All linguistic aspects of the play have to be taken into consideration. Special attention should also be paid to prosodic features, since 'the dialogue will be characterized by rhythm, intonation patterns, pitch and loudness, all elements that may not be immediately apparent from a straightforward reading of the written text in isolation' (Bassnett McGuire 1991a: 122).

Adaptation and domestication are usually the most frequent techniques used in translating drama since 'adaptation is sometimes regarded as a form of translation which is characteristic of particular genre, most notably, drama' (Bastin 2009: 4). Adaptation is also viewed as a 'reterritorialization' of the original work and an 'annexation' in the name of the audience of the new version (Brisset 1986: 10, quoted in Baker 2009).

Adaptation is defined as a set of translative interventions which result in a text that is not generally accepted as a translation but is nevertheless recognised as representing a ST. It involves the following adaptation procedures (Bastin 2009: 4–5):

1. Transcription of the original or word-for-word reproduction of part of the text in the original language, usually accompanied by literal translation.
2. Omission: the elimination or implication of part of the text.
3. Expansion: the addition or explication of source information either in the body or in footnotes or a glossary.
4. Exoticism: substitution of stretches of slang, dialect, nonsense word, etc. in the original text by rough equivalent in the TL.
5. Updating: the replacement of outdated or obscure information by modern equivalents.
6. Situational or cultural adequacy: the recreation of a context that is more familiar or culturally appropriate from the target reader's perspective than the one used in the original.
7. Creation: a more global replacement of the original text with a text that preserves only the essential message/ideas/functions of the original.

Adaptation could be caused by (ibid.):

1. Cross-code breakdown where no lexical equivalents exist between the SL and TL especially when translating meta-language.
2. Situational or cultural inadequacy where the context or views referred to in the original do not exist or apply in the target culture.
3. Genre switches: a change from one discourse type to another.
4. Disruption of the communication process: a new epoch or approach or the need to address different readership.

These conditions cause two types of adaptation: a local one applying to some parts of the original texts and caused by internal factors without affecting it as a whole, and a global one that is determined by factors outside the text and which affects the text as a whole.

The following extracts from *Pygmalion* by George Bernard Shaw have been translated into Arabic using adaptation. Names of characters and places have been replaced by Arabic names.

THE FLOWER GIRL:
[taking advantage of the military gentleman's proximity to establish friendly relations with him.] If it's worse it's a sign it's nearly over. So cheer up, Captain; and buy a flower off a poor girl.

THE GENTLEMAN:
I'm sorry, I haven't any change.

THE FLOWER GIRL:
I can give you change, Captain,

THE GENTLEMAN:
For a sovereign? I've nothing less.

THE FLOWER GIRL:
Garn! Oh do buy a flower off me, Captain. I can change half-a-crown.

بياعة الورد (تستغل قرب الشرطي منها لتلطف الجو معه): لو كانت أسوا معنتاها رح تخلص, خلاص يا باشا فرفش واشتري وردة من البنت المسكينة

الزلمة المحترم: متأسف فش معي فراطة

بياعة الورد: بصرفلك يا باشا

الزلمة المحترم: ليش؟ عشان تذكار, معيش غيره

بياعة الورد: وبعدين! أنا معاي فراطة نص ليرة

Notice here that the names as well as the currency have been adapted to suit the target audience. Since the theme of the play is how to teach a lady to speak properly, standard Arabic would not have been a good choice. The colloquial gives more room for the flower girl to use a variety of utterances associated with a low social status.

11.1 Translate the following extracts from the same play employing both adaptation and domestication.

THE SARCASTIC ONE:
[amazed] Well, who said I didn't? Bly me!* You know everything, you do.

THE FLOWER GIRL:
[still nursing her sense of injury] Ain't no call to meddle with me, he ain't.

THE BYSTANDER:
[to her] Of course he ain't. Don't you stand it from him. [To the note taker] See here: what call have you to know about people what never offered to meddle with you? Where's your warrant?

SEVERAL BYSTANDERS:
[encouraged by this seeming point of law] Yes: where's your warrant?

THE FLOWER GIRL:
Let him say what he likes. I don't want to have no truck with him.

THE BYSTANDER:
You take us for dirt under your feet, don't you? Catch you taking liberties with a gentleman!

THE SARCASTIC BYSTANDER:
Yes: tell him where he comes from if you want to go fortune-telling.

THE NOTE TAKER:
Cheltenham, Harrow, Cambridge, and India.

Pygmalion, George Bernard Shaw, Act 1

http://classiclit.about.com/library/bl-etexts/gbshaw/bl-gbshaw-pyg-1.htm (accessed 31 May 2011)

*Bly me: usually spelled 'blimey' = a Cockney exclamation of surprise (reduced form of 'God blind me')

11.2 *Translate the following from the same play using at least three adaptation procedures.*

HIGGINS: I was going to India to meet you.

PICKERING: Where do you live?

HIGGINS: 27A Wimpole Street. Come and see me tomorrow.

PICKERING: I'm at the Carlton. Come with me now and let's have a jaw over some supper.

HIGGINS: Right you are.

THE FLOWER GIRL [to Pickering, as he passes her]: Buy a flower, kind gentleman. I'm short for my lodging.

PICKERING: I really haven't any change. I'm sorry [he goes away].

HIGGINS [shocked at girl's mendacity]: Liar. You said you could change half-a-crown.

THE FLOWER GIRL [rising in desperation]: You ought to be stuffed with nails, you ought. [Flinging the basket at his feet]: Take the whole blooming basket for sixpence.

http://classiclit.about.com/library/bl-etexts/gbshaw/bl-gbshaw-pyg-1.htm (accessed 31 May 2011)

....
....
....
....
....
....
....
....
....
....
....
....
....
....

11.3 Translate the following lines from Shakespeare's Macbeth *taking the prosodic features into consideration while translating.*

Tomorrow, and tomorrow, and tomorrow,
Creeps in this petty pace from day to day,
To the last syllable of recorded time;
And all our yesterdays have lighted fools
The way to dusty death. Out, out, brief candle!
Life's but a walking shadow, a poor player
That struts and frets his hour upon the stage

....
....
....
....
....
....
....

....
....
....
....
....

11.4 Translate the following from Arabic into English applying adaptation.

سعاد: امشي من هنا. تبيع الماء في حي السقايين؟

سعيد: واذا ما مشيت ؟

سعاد: ثكلتك امك.

سعيد: كنت ارغب بالحديث معك.

سعاد: وانا لا ارغب. سأذهب الان

سعيد: مع ستين سلامة .

....
....
....
....
....
....
....
....

LESSON 12: POETRY

Poetry is a literary genre that has its distinctive and challenging features. Perhaps it is thought to be the most challenging to the translator. What distinguishes poetry from other genres is its reliance on figurative language, rhyme and rhythm. To be a poet is to deviate from the usual linguistic norm of expression. To deviate is to be able to play with words and twist them to suit your needs. Such foregrounding strategies employed by poets put a lot of pressure on the translator, especially when the two languages are linguistically and culturally distant as is the case with Arabic and English. Before initiating the translation task, you should read the SL poem carefully, understand it and read about the poet, his or her ideology and most frequent metaphors, since each poet has his or her own diction that can be elicited from reading more than one poem. This will give you a basis and a direction in the translation.

Strategies for translating poetry

Various scholars have emphasised the fact that poetry is a special kind of language that requires particular translation strategies. The following could be implemented (Bassnett-McGuire 1980: 81–2):

1. Phonemic translation: attempts to recreate the sounds of the SL in the TL, transferring the meaning at the same time.
2. Literal translation: involves word-for-word translation.
3. Metrical translation: reproduces the original meter into the TL.
   This strategy is not always successful since each language has its own metrical structure.
4. Verse-to-prose translation: producing the TL as prose instead of the ST which is a poem. This method has some weaknesses, the biggest of which is the loss of the beauty of the original poem, or the beauty of the poetic shape.
5. Rhymed translation emphasises transferring the rhyme of the original poem to TL. The result will be appropriate phonetically but tends to be semantically inappropriate.
6. Free verse translation. With this method the translator may be able to achieve the accurate equivalents in the TL at the expense of the literary value.

It has become clear that poetry is a difficult genre because it is a condensed form of language that is rich with meaning. In addition, poetry applies imagery and the use of figures of speech, especially metaphor, which makes poetry even more challenging for the translator. The following procedures for translating metaphors could be used (Newmark 1988b: 88–95):

1. Reproducing the same image in the TL.
2. Replacing the image in the SL with a standard TL image.
3. Translating metaphors as similes.
4. Translating metaphors (or similes) as similes plus sense.

5. Conversion of metaphor into sense (explanation).
6. Deletion.
7. Translating the same metaphor, but combined with sense.

12.1 Identify the strategies used in translating the following poem.

When You Are Old and Grey
By William Butler Yeats

When you are old and grey and full of sleep,
And nodding by the fire, take down this book,
And slowly read, and dream of the soft look
Your eyes had once, and of their shadows deep;

How many loved your moments of glad grace,
And loved your beauty with love false or true,
But one man loved the pilgrim soul in you,
And loved the sorrows of your changing face;

Arabic translation

عندما تكبر ويشتعل رأسك شيبا

تترنح نعسا أمام النار

خذ هذا الكتاب

أقرا ببطء وتذكر كم رأت عيونك؟

كم أحبك من ناس وأحبوا صحبتك

كم أحبوا جمالك

وكم كان صادقا أم كاذبا ذلك الحب

ولكن هنالك شخص واحد أحب روح الحاج فيك

وأحب حزن وجهك المتغير

12.2 Identify figures of speech in the poem below by Alfred, Lord Tennyson and decide on the best strategy to translate them into Arabic.

....

....

....

....

....

Tears, Idle Tears
By Alfred, Lord Tennyson
Tears, idle tears, I know not what they mean,
Tears from the depth of some divine despair
Rise in the heart, and gather to the eyes,
In looking on the happy Autumn-fields,
And thinking of the days that are no more.

Fresh as the first beam glittering on a sail,
That brings our friends up from the underworld,
Sad as the last which reddens over one
That sinks with all we love below the verge;
So sad, so fresh, the days that are no more.

Ah, sad and strange as in dark summer dawns
The earliest pipe of half-awakened birds
To dying ears, when unto dying eyes
The casement slowly grows a glimmering square;
So sad, so strange, the days that are no more.

Dear as remembered kisses after death,
And sweet as those by hopeless fancy feigned
On lips that are for others; deep as love,
Deep as first love, and wild with all regret;
O Death in Life, the days that are no more.

http://www.online-literature.com/donne/729/ (accessed 31 May 2011)

Glossary

Despair	يأس	Regret	ندم
Glittering	تتلألأ	Feigned	مختلق
Casement	نافذة		

12.3   *Now translate the poem.*

....

....

....

....

....

....

....

....

....

....

....

....

....

....

....

....

....

....

....

....

....

....

....

....

....

....

....

....

12.4   Translate the following lines by the Tunisian poet Al-Shabbi and identify the strategies that you use.

فلا بد ان يستجيب القدر	اذا الشعب يوما اراد الحياة
ولا بد للقيد ان ينكسر	ولا بد لليل ان ينجلي
يعش ابد الدهر بين الحفر	ومن لا يحب صعود الجبال

....

....

....

....

....

....

MODULE REVIEW EXERCISES

1. *Translate the following text following the most appropriate strategy.*

Looking at the gleaming, bulging pods slung under their wingtip pylons, Roger had a premature inkling of the fires that waited within, a frigid terror that echoed the siren wail of the air raid warnings. He'd sucked nervously on his ice cream and gripped his father's hand tightly while the band ripped through a cheerful Sousa March and only forgot his fear when a flock of Thunder chiefs sliced by overhead and rattled the car windows for miles around.

He has the same feeling now, as an adult reading this intelligence assessment that he had as a child, watching the nuclear powered bombers sleeping in their concrete beds.

http://www.infinityplus.co.uk/stories/colderwar.htm (accessed 19 April 2011)

....

....

....

....

....

....

....

....

....

2. *Identify figures of speech in the following poem.*

To a Skylark
By Percy Bysshe Shelley

Hail to thee, blithe Spirit!
Bird thou never wert,
That from heaven, or near it,
Pourest thy full heart
In profuse strains of unpremeditated art.

Higher still and higher
From the earth thou springest
Like a cloud of fire;
The blue deep thou wingest,
And singing still dost soar, and soaring ever singest.
In the golden lightning
Of the sunken sun,
O'er which clouds are bright'ning,
Thou dost float and run,
Like an unbodied joy whose race is just begun.
The pale purple even
Melts around thy flight;
Like a star of heaven
In the broad daylight
Thou art unseen, but yet I hear thy shrill delight –
Keen as are the arrows
Of that silver sphere
Whose intense lamp narrows
In the white dawn clear
Until we hardly see – we feel that it is there.
All the earth and air
With thy voice is loud,
As, when night is bare,
From one lonely cloud
The moon rains out her beams, and heaven is overflowed.

http://www.netpoets.com/classic/poems/057025.htm (accessed 31 May 2011)

---

3. *Discuss the most appropriate strategies to translate the figures of speech you identified.*

....

....

....

....

4. *Translate the poem and discuss your translation with a colleague.*

Glossary

Spirit	روح	**Rainbow**	قوس قزح
Unpremeditated	عفوي	**Melody**	الحان
Springest	يرتفع	**Scattering**	ينثر
Shrill	صاخب	**Fears**	مخاوف

....

....

....

....

....

....

....

....

....

....

5. *Translate the following excerpt applying domestication.*

Driver

Passenger! (Passenger climbs into the cab. Driver sings.) Hello, hello, and welcome to this yellow cab, hello, hello, yellow, hello. All our drivers belong to the union, so you won't be driven by a scab, hello and welcome to this yellow cab! (speaking) Hello and thank you for riding yellow cabs. Here is your free complimentary yellow cabbage. (Driver tosses a yellow cabbage to Passenger. Passenger starts to get out of the cab. Driver pulls him back in.) Off we go! And where would you like to go.

http://drama.eserver.org/plays/contemporary/philosophy-and-cabbage.html   (accessed 21 October 2013)

....

....

....

....

....

....

....

....

....

....

---

6. *Translate the following text from Arabic applying foreignisation.*

شعبان : ليس اليوم فقط .. كل يوم أنا على هذا الحال يرد لي في المتوسط نحو ثلاثين ملفاً فلا يهدأ لي بال ، ولا يطمئن لي خاطر ، ولا يرضى لي ضمير ، حتى أنكب عليها انكباباً ، وأعمل فيها بكل قوتي وهمتي ، إلى أن أنجزها ، وأفرغ منها .. وأجلس بعدها كما ترى ، خالياً مرتاحاً ، أشرب قهوتي ، وأدخن سيجارتي بلذة ، ومتعة .. وقد أديت واجبي على أكمل وجه، وبأسرع وقت

مرسي : (بدون وعي) حمار!!

شعبان : (مأخوذا ماذا تقول ؟

مرسي : لا تؤاخذني يا "شعبان" إنما أنا أرثي لك ، ولقد وضعت يدي الآن على سر خيبتك.

http://www.maqola.org/521 (accessed 21 October 2013)

....

....

....

....

....

....

....

Economics Texts

Economics is a discipline that is related to the study of production and consumption as well as transfer of wealth. It is subdivided into microeconomics, which deals with industries and economic activities on the individual level, and macroeconomics, which is the study of the economics of the entire country or the international market. There is an increased need for the translation of economics texts due to globalisation and the proliferation of companies worldwide. This has led to more cooperation and partnership between business organisations internationally, more translations made for documents related to loans, purchasing shares and establishing multinational companies. Economic translation is required for marketing and commerce, banking and the investment sector, the insurance industry, accounting and auditing, and marketing research. It deals with various types of documents such as business plans, blocks of tender documents, invoices, account statements, consignment bills, offers, credit requests, guarantee letters, feasibility reports, audit reports, other financial reports and many other documents of economic use.

Features of economic discourse

Though economics is related to everyday language, it has its own linguistic features:

> sometimes the jargon of a specialist group seeps into the common language of the wider community. This is particularly likely to happen where the activities of that sub-group are fashionable or impinge directly on the life of the wider community. (Katamba 2004: 168)

Economic texts often present visual information linguistically, making use of mathematical systems to represent economic facts. For instance, they may use mathematical symbols, segmental diagrams and tabular information, and other visual data (statistical tables, maps and graphs). The language of economics in particular relies on grammatical structures (e.g. conditionals, passive structures, relative clauses and logical connectives) and rhetorical functions (e.g. assumption, hypothesis, prediction, explanation and generalisation).

Economic discourse is a global discourse. This globalisation has led to the emergence of many loan words. In English economic discourse, these loan words are mainly taken from French, Italian, German, Japanese, Greek and Spanish. 'The enterprising spirit of the English people and their fondness for travel and colonization, as well as the great development of their commerce, have brought in miscellaneous words from every quarter of the world' Greenough and Kittredge 2001: 108).

Translation problems and strategies

Translating economic texts is demanding since translators must stick to the information in the SL. The whole document should be translated without leaving anything out. Figures and numbers, for example, should be given utmost attention, and no new numbers should be added, changed or removed. Another problem is related to false cognates or 'false friends'. These are the words that look alike but have partially or completely different meanings in different languages, e.g. compare *become* in English with *bekommen* in German, which means 'to get' not 'to become'. These words are also related to neologism as explained below.

LESSON 13: NEOLOGISM

Neologism is considered one of the most common challenges for translators of economic texts. It is defined as 'newly coined lexical units or existing lexical units that acquire new sense' (Newmark 1988a: 140). New terms are continuously being created and translators often cannot find available translations for them so they have to come up with their own. Newmark (ibid. pp. 140–51) proposes twelve types of neologisms and different translation strategies for each type. They are classified into two main categories, the first referred to as existing lexical items but with a new sense. This category is subdivided into words and collocations. Translation strategies suggested for them include transference with inverted commas, TL neologisms with composites, and TL derived words. The second category of neologisms covers the new terms introduced in the TL and they are subdivided into the following: new coinages, derived words, abbreviations, collocations, eponyms, phrasal words, transferred words, acronyms, pseudo-neologisms and internationalisms. Strategies to deal with this category include: naturalisation, recognised TL translation, functional terms, descriptive terms, literal translation and translation procedure combination.

13.1 Translate the following text, paying attention to numbers and figures.

Uranium Purchases and Prices

Owners and operators of U.S. civilian nuclear power reactors ('civilian owner/operators' or 'COOs') purchased a total of 55 million pounds U3O8e (equivalent) of deliveries from U.S. suppliers and foreign suppliers during 2011, at a weighted-average price of $55.64 per pound U3O8e. The 2011 total of 55 million pounds U3O8e increased 18 percent compared with the 2010 total of 47 million pounds U3O8e. (Uranium quantities are expressed in the unit of measure U3O8e (equivalent)). U3O8e is uranium oxide (or uranium concentrate) and the equivalent uranium-component of hexafluoride (UF6) and enriched uranium. Nine percent of the U3O8e delivered in 2011 was U.S.-origin uranium at a weighted-average price of $52.12 per pound. Foreign-origin uranium accounted for the remaining 91 percent of deliveries at a weighted average price of $55.98 per pound. Australian-origin and Canadian-origin uranium together accounted for 31 percent of the 55 million pounds. Uranium originating in Kazakhstan, Russia and Uzbekistan accounted for 40 percent, and the remaining 20 percent originated from Brazil, China, Malawi, Namibia, Niger, South Africa, and Ukraine. Owners and operators of U.S. civilian nuclear power reactors purchased uranium for 2011 deliveries from 32 sellers, up from the 23 sellers in 2010.

http://205.254.135.7/uranium/marketing/pdf/2011umar.pdf (accessed 28 May 2011)

Glossary

Nuclear power reactors	مفاعلات الطاقة النووية	Foreign-origin	اجنبي المنشأ
Uranium oxide	اكسيد اليورانيوم	Civilian	مدني
Enriched uranium	اليورانيوم المخصب		

....

....

....

....

....

....

....

....

....

....

....

 13.2 *Translate the following text paying attention to false cognates in English and Arabic.*

An almost universal feature of most economies is the coexistence of 'base' and 'broad' money instruments. In modern economies, the monetary base consists of small denomination government paper notes, while broad money consists of electronic book-entry credits created by the banking system redeemable in base money. In earlier historical episodes, the monetary base often consisted of specie (gold or silver coins) with broad money consisting of privately-issued banknotes redeemable in base money. In this chapter, we consider a set of simple models designed to help us think about the determinants of such monetary arrangements.

www.sfu.ca/~dandolfa/macro2005.pdf (accessed 28 May 2011)

 Glossary

Monetary base	الأساس النقدي	Paper notes	اوراق نقدية
Denomination	فئة	Banknotes	اوراق مصرفية

....

....

....

....

....

....

....

....

13.3 *Identify and translate the neologisms in the following blog.*

EXECUTIVE compensation, and especially the big bonuses that characterised Wall Street pay in recent years, has come in for a great deal of criticism as financial markets have melted down – particularly given the massive government aid many financial institutions have received. Bail-outs have frequently come with strings attached, limiting or advising against lavish pay packages. But so far, little progress has been made on attempts to claw back bonuses already paid, to traders earning millions of dollars while their desks approached the precipice. But on this score, UBS is proving itself quite innovative:

> 'Just as bonuses (Latin for "good") are paid out for good performance, maluses ("bad") will be meted out if the bank subsequently makes losses or if the employee misses performance targets, UBS said. The maluses could wipe out all previously agreed share bonuses and two thirds of all cash bonuses under stringent new rules designed to align the interests of executives and traders with those of shareholders.'

I'd say that the primary result of such a rule would likely be the quick departure from UBS of anyone able to find work elsewhere, but the *Times* story quoted above notes that UBS is pulling out the legal stops to see if it can hand 'maluses' to employees who have already left the firm.

http://www.economist.com/blogs/freeexchange/2008/11/more_financial_neologisms (accessed 28 May 2011)

Glossary

Financial markets	الأسواق المالية	Shareholders	اصحاب الاسهم
Interests	مصالح	Bonus	مكافأة نقدية
Traders	تجار		

....

....

....

....

....

....

....

....

....

....

LESSON 14: METAPHORS IN ECONOMIC DISCOURSE

Another problem in economic discourse is related to the use of figures of speech, puns and polysemes. Economic discourse makes use of metaphors. Metaphors used in economic texts are classified into three types. The first type is used for textual decoration or illustration, referred to as *image metaphors*. The second type is the *generic-level metaphor* which occurs generally in the language. The third type is the *specific-level metaphor* which is used to explain specific economic problems (Henderson 1982). The following strategies are suggested to translate metaphors (Dobrzyńska 1995: 595):

1. Using an exact equivalent of the original metaphor.
2. Using another metaphorical phrase which would express a similar sense.
3. Replacing an untranslatable metaphor of the original with its approximate literal paraphrase.

14.1 *Identify metaphors in the following excerpts from an article in* The Economist.

The euro-zone crisis

Fighting for its life

The euro zone is in intensive care

WHAT'S the French for "this sucker could go down"? Echoes of 2008, when the global financial system wobbled and George Bush gave his pithy view of the American economy, now resound on the other side of the Atlantic. Credit-default-swap spreads for European banks, a measure of how costly it is to buy insurance against their default, are at record highs ...

The rates that banks charge each other for loans in the interbank market are rising, too, as they did then. Rumours swirl and panic flares: shares in BNP Paribas, a well-run French bank, dropped by 12% on the morning of September 13th following reports that no one would lend it dollars. BNP's denials saw the shares bounce back later in the day. Shares in Société Générale, another French bank, whipsawed too. The French banks' reliance on short-term dollar funding, which American money-market funds are increasingly leery of providing, is one reason why Moody's, a ratings agency, downgraded Société Générale on September 14th, though exposure to sovereign default is also a key factor.

The government at the heart of concerns again this week is that of Greece. Panicked officials are racing to plug a gaping hole in the budget and accelerate reforms in the face of speculation that international lenders will withhold the next €8 billion tranche of the country's bail-out. If the funds are not released within two weeks, the government risks being unable to pay wages and pensions. A hastily announced property tax should raise about €2 billion, which may just keep the budget deficit below 9% of GDP this year.

http://www.economist.com/node/21529044 (accessed 28 May 2011)

Glossary

Insurance	تأمين	Downgraded	خفضت ائتمان
Loans	قروض	Budget	ميزانية
Shares	اسهم	Tax	ضريبة
Short-term	قصيرة الأجل	Deficit	عجز

14.2 *Now translate the text using the most appropriate strategy.*

....

....

....

....

....

....

....

....

....

....

....

....

....

....

....

....

....

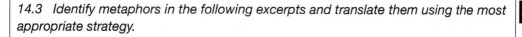

14.3   *Identify metaphors in the following excerpts and translate them using the most appropriate strategy.*

سماء أوروبا ملبدة بغيوم اليورو. وتوقعات باستمرار الأزمة حتى 2013

أزمة اليونان.. وشبح الخروج

ومن الجدير هنا ان نشير إلى أن شبح الخروج من منطقة اليورو لم يكن يلاحق إسبانيا فحسب، بل سبقتها بأيام قليلة جارتها ''اليونان''، والتي قالت حكومتها أوائل يونيو الجاري بأن وزارة المالية أقرت مساعدة قدرها 81 مليار يورو لأكبر أربعة من بنوكها، لتؤهل بذلك البنوك المتعثرة للحصول مجددا على تمويل من البنك المركزى الأوروبى، في خطوة منها لتحقيق نوع من الاستقرار لقاعدة رأس المال التى استنفدت تقريبا لبنوك ناشيونال بنك وألفا ويوروبنك وبيريوس.. وقالت الوزّارة حينها: ''هذا الضخ لرأس المال يعيد مستويات كفاية رأس المال لدى هذه البنوك ويضمن لها القدرة على الوصول للتمويل النقدى من البنك المركزى الأوروبى''.

http://www.businesstendersmag.com/ar (accessed 4 August 2013)

....

....

....

....

....

....

....

....

....

....

....

....

....

....

LESSON 15: TERMINOLOGY: MARKETING

Terminology is a challenging issue especially for the non-professional translator. A number of terms have specific meanings in economics but are vague and general in everyday language. This problem could be dealt with once the translator has decided on the most appropriate dictionary to use. The text has to be scanned first so that the translator can decide on the basic economic genre being dealt with. Specific terms are identified and translated using specialised dictionaries before the translator starts the actual translation process. Knowledge of the discipline can undoubtedly facilitate the process of understanding economic terminologies, and rigorous training in translating economic texts can be very beneficial to the translator, equipping him or her with the translation terminologies, as well as the relevant strategies to deal with this text type.

Marketing terminology is mainly found in the translation of brochures, catalogues, offers, advertisements, web pages, marketing and business reports, marketing news and business articles, and business correspondence in general.

 15.1 *Translate the following marketing extract into English. Then specify a list of the marketing terminologies used.*

التسويق الشبكي وتعرف أيضا بالتجارة الشبكية أو البيع المباشر، هو المصطلح الذي يصف هيكل التسويق التي تستخدمها بعض الشركات كجزء من استراتيجيتها الشاملة للتسويق. هيكل مصمم لإنشاء قوة في التسويق والمبيعات عن طريق إمكانية الربح للمروجين لمنتجات الشركة من خلال ترويجهم، ليس فقط من خلال المبيعات الشخصية المباشرة، ولكن أيضا بالنسبة للمبيعات من المروجين الآخرين الذين التحقوا بالعمل عن طريقهم، وخلق شبكة من الموزعين والتسلسل الشبكي للمستويات المتعددة للربح في شكل شبكي.

http://ar.wikipedia.org/wiki (accessed 5 August 2013)

....

....

....

....

....

15.2 *Translate the following English advert into Arabic and discuss its discourse features with the class.*

What is Orange E-Shop?
It is the first online telecom E-Shop hosting a wide variety of our products and services that you can purchase with a simple click of a button.

What can I find here?
Here you can buy any product or service that you desire from the below lines:
– Mobile handsets
– Pay monthly mobile plans
– Mobile handsets with pay monthly mobile plans
– ADSL offers
– Pay monthly and cost control Internet Everywhere wireless internet subscriptions
– Pay as you go Internet Everywhere wireless internet subscriptions

Do you sell pay as you go lines for mobile subscriptions?
No, currently we are not selling any mobile pay as you go offers through E-Shop and this item might be sold in the future.

How can I buy any of the products featured on E-Shop?
Buying a product through E-Shop is very simple, all you need to do is following the below steps:
– Click on the "buy" button after choosing the product you would like to get
– After reviewing your order and the price to be paid, click on "next"
– Fill in the form that appears to you with your personal details and put a check mark next to "I have read and understood the terms and conditions" then click on next
– Validate your order information and price then click on "submit"

What are the next steps to get my order?
– An E-mail will be sent to you summarizing your order
– You will be contacted by our sales team confirming your order and residence information
– You will be contacted again in order to be given the address of the closest shop to your address where you can find your order prepared and ready for pick up

Do you offer an online payment and delivery options through your E-Shop?
No, these options will be featured soon on E-Shop

http://www.orange.jo/sites/Residential/English/HelpAndSupport/Pages/eshop-faqs.aspx
(accessed 20 October 2013)

....

....

....

....

....

....

....

....

....

....

15.3 Translate the following advertisement in Arabic and discuss its discourse features with the class.

عروض تجارية لم تشاهدها من قبل .. شاهد الان اقوى المشاريع والصفقات الاستثمارية

فرصة رائعة للمستثمرين ورجال الاعمال

عروض وصفقات رابحة وخدمات الاستشارات من خبير ومستشار دولي في مجال الاستثمارات

الان اطلق العنان لاستثماراتك وزد ارباحك وانطلق بهمة نحو القمة .

لماذا ترضى بالقليل ان كان بمقدورك ان تجني الكثير .. اغتنم فرصتك واستثمر اموالك في مجالات اثبتت
جدواها وعلو قدمها على كثير من المجالات الاستثمارية الاخرى حتى لقبها البعض بـ المشاريع الذهبية
لماذا تنتظر القليل والكثير هنا بانتظارك .

http://twitmail.com/email/59076986/1350 (accessed 20 October 2013)

....

....

....

....

....

....

....

....

....

LESSON 16: TERMINOLOGY: INVESTMENT

Investment discourse is used for companies with regard to benefits returned from various purchases. It covers various business documents such as contracts, agreements and documents related to insurance (health insurance, life insurance, car insurance, insurance of machinery and electronic sales, etc.). Investment written discourse is highly formal and is usually characterised by the use of passive, short sentences, use of directives and legal terminology. Accuracy is a very important issue that should be taken into consideration because any mistake in translation might have serious legal consequences.

16.1 Translate the following extracts from an insurance agreement. Pay attention to the grammatical structures and try to use the most appropriate grammatical forms.

INSURANCE SERVICES FRAMEWORK AGREEMENT
Dated: 26 August 2004, effective from 1 January 2004

BETWEEN:
(1) **Norwich Union Customer Services (Singapore) Pte Ltd,** a company registered in Singapore with registration number 200303457R and whose registered office is at 4 Shenton Way, #27-02 SGX Centre 2, Singapore 068807 (the **"Client"**); and
(2) **Exlservice Holdings, Inc.** a company registered in the State of Delaware and whose principal office is at 350 Park Avenue, 10 th Floor, New York, NY 10022 (**"EXL Holdings (US)"**).

1 DEFINITIONS AND INTERPRETATION
1.1 In this Agreement, unless inconsistent with the context or otherwise specified, the definitions set out in schedule 1 shall apply.
1.2 References to clauses and schedules are to clauses of and the schedules to this Agreement.
1.3 The schedules form part of this Agreement and have the same force and effect as if expressly set out in the body of this Agreement.
1.4 References to paragraphs are to the paragraphs of an Insurance Services Work Order.
1.5 Words importing gender include each gender.
1.6 References to persons include bodies corporate, firms and unincorporated associations and that person's legal personal representatives and successors.
1.7 The singular includes the plural and vice versa.

....
....
....
....
....

....
....
....
....
....
....
....

2 INSURANCE SERVICES WORK ORDERS

2.1 Where the Client and EXL Holdings (US) agree to enter into a contract for the provision of services (which may include the provision of equipment and other assets), the Parties shall, subject to clause 2.3, complete an Insurance Services Work Order. For the avoidance of doubt, only Vicar Talwar and Rohit Kapoor, or such other persons who have been specifically identified to Client by EXL Holdings (US), shall be authorised to sign any Insurance Services Work Orders on behalf of EXL Holdings (US).

....
....
....
....
....
....
....
....
....

3 THE SERVICES

3.1 EXL Holdings (US) shall supply each of the Insurance Services as set out in an Insurance Services Work Order to the Client in accordance with the terms of this Agreement and the Insurance Services Work Order.

3.2 Subject to the Contract Change Control Procedures EXL Holdings (US) and the Client shall comply with the agreed Project Timetable set out in the applicable Insurance Services Work Order.

3.3 Where the Client is under an obligation to pass on the Insurance Services to an Authorised Agent, Associated Company or Authorised User, EXL Holdings (US) shall as directed by the Client, supply the Insurance Services so that Client can pass them on or procure that they are passed on to that Authorised Agent, Associated Company or Authorised User as the case may be provided that the obligations of EXL Holdings (US) in respect thereof shall be to Client and not the Authorised Agent, Associated Company or Authorised User. The Client shall procure that such

Authorised Agent, Authorised Company or Authorised User shall, as necessary, comply with the obligations of the Client hereunder. For the avoidance of doubt, it is expressly understood that Client shall be responsible for the payment of the charges.

http://contracts.onecle.com/exlservice/norwich.svc.2004.08.26.shtml (accessed 29 May 2011)

Glossary

Agreement	اتفاق	Assets	اصول الشركة
Insurance Services	خدمات تأمين	Procedures	اجراءات
Representatives	ممثلين	Comply with	يستجيب ل
Authorised to sign	مخول بالتوقيع	Procure	يتدبر

....
....
....
....
....
....
....
....
....
....

16.2 *Translate the following phrases into English.*

1. الأضرار المادية والثاني هو المسؤولية المدنية. ....

2. مبلغ التحمل . ...

3. الإستهلاك العادي ....

4. الخسائر التبعية ....

16.3 *Translate the following extracts from an Arabic insurance agreement.*

من المعلوم ان الوثيقة تقسم إلى قسمين: القسم الأول هو الأضرار المادية والثاني هو المسؤولية المدنية تجاه الغير ولكل قسم إستثناءاته.

القسم الأول الإستثناءات الخاصة بقسم (الأضرار المادية):

1. مبلغ التحمل و هو المبلغ أو النسبة التى يتحملها المؤمن له في كل حادث أو خسارة
2. الخسائر التبعية بكافة صورها المادية و الغرامات التى تعرض على المقاول بسبب التأخير في إنجاز العمل و اكتماله في المدة المحددة بموجب عقد المقاولة.
3. الخسائر و الأضرار التى تنشا من عيوب التصميم.
4. تكاليف استبدال أو إصلاح أو تصحيح المواد المعيبة أو العمالة المعيبة
5. الإستهلاك العادي و التآكل و الصدأ و التأكسد و التلف نتيجة عدم الاستعمال أو نتيجة العوامل الجوية العادي.

http://www.insurance4arab.com/2012/10/blog-post_1617.html (accessed 4 August 2103)

....

....

....

....

....

....

....

LESSON 17: TERMINOLOGY: BANKING

Banking discourse involves the translation of annual reports, prospectuses, bank statements, investment marketing translation, macroeconomic survey translation, equity research translation, shareholder information, profit and loss reports, insurance policy translation, as well as banking, finance, and insurance websites. What distinguishes banking discourse from other economic discourse types is its heavy reliance on figures and statistics. Making use of TL-relevant templates facilitates the translation process by giving the translator more time to concentrate on the linguistic message to be conveyed rather than wasting time looking for a suitable presentation method.

17.1 Translate the following Arabic and English extracts from account-opening forms using the most appropriate terminology.

> Please complete ALL relevant areas on the form in BLOCK LETTERS. If you are applying for a Joint Account, please complete both applicants' details. You are required to submit to us all relevant information stated in the Checklist under section VIII with your application.
>
> For Joint Account Only
>
> We, the undersigned, hereby agree that the signature of any one of us on or in relation to any matter regarding the joint account will bind the other joint-account holders and expressly constitute an authorisation for each joint-account holder to have full powers to conduct any transaction on the joint account by way of instruction to the Bank and other instructions to operate the joint account including but not limited to notice of change in information declared at this form without requiring our joint signatures. We have read and understood the provisions relevant to joint account in the General Terms and Conditions of HSBC Bank (Vietnam) Ltd. and agree to be bound by them.
>
> https://www.hsbc.com.vn/1/PA_ES_Content_Mgmt/content/vietnam/pdf_app/html/ AOF_EN_20Jul.pdf (accessed 21October 2013)

....

....

....

....

....

....

....

....

....

....

....

....

....

....

....

التسجيل وفتح الحساب

لغرض تنفيذ هذه الاتفاقية ، يقوم الزبون بفتح:

حساب إستثمار لدى قسم الوساطة التابع لبنك مسقط يودع فيه الزبون مبالغ لشراء أوراق مالية، وسيقوم قسم الوساطة التابع لبنك مسقط بإضافة المبالغ العائدة من بيع أي أوراق مالية مباعة من قبل الزبون من خلال خدمة بنك مسقط دايركت في هذا الحساب (حساب تداول أوراق مالية مع قسم الوساطة التابع لبنك مسقط).

http://brokerage.bankmuscat.com/Uploads/Downloads/Brokerage-Account-Opening-Form.pdf (accessed 21 October 2013)

....

....

....

....

....

....

....

....

 17.2   *Translate the following description of profit and loss statement into Arabic.*

What is a profit and loss statement?

The profit and loss statement is a summary of the financial performance of a business over time (monthly, quarterly or annually is most common). It reflects the past performance of the business and is the report most often used by small business owners to track how their business is performing.

As the name indicates the profit and loss statement (also known as a statement of financial performance or an income statement) measures the profit or loss of a business over a specified period. A profit and loss statement summarises the income for a period and subtracts the expenses incurred for the same period to calculate the profit or loss for the business.

Traders, partnerships and small proprietary companies are not required to prepare and lodge a profit and loss statement with their annual tax return. However, they are very useful in helping you to objectively determine the financial performance of your business. Most accounting software packages will produce a profit and loss statement, but you may need the help of a bookkeeper or an accountant unless your business is very small.

All public companies and large proprietary companies are required by law to prepare a formal financial report that complies with Australian Accounting Standards for each financial year.

http://www.smallbusiness.wa.gov.au/understanding-profit-loss-statements/#profit-and-loss (accessed 15 April 2013)

....

....

....

....

....

....

....

....

....

....

....

....

....

....

....

....

....

....

....

....

....

17.3 *Translate the following news report.*

UK manufacturing growth slows

01 May 2012 – 09:38

UK manufacturing growth faltered in April as exports were hit by weaker demand from across the globe.

Markit's Purchasing Managers' Index registered 50.5 in April compared to 51.9 in March.

Any number over 50 on the index denotes growth with today's figures showing output rising at slowest rate of the year so far.

Consensus forecasts were for an expansion of 51.6.

However, it was the fifth month in a row that the manufacturing sector reported expansion.

New export orders fell at their steepest pace since May 2009 pushing total orders down slightly for first time in five months.

The drop in exports resulted from weaker demand from mainland Europe, the US and East Asia, Markit said.

After surging higher on the back of rising oil prices during March the latest figures showed an easing in cost inflationary pressures.

Companies nonetheless continued to report paying higher prices for chemicals, eggs, feedstock, fuel, metals, oil and polymers, Markit said.

A number of companies also indicated that suppliers were raising their charges to reflect increased transport costs.

More of a worry for policy-makers was a continued acceleration in average output price inflation in April.

Charges rose at the quickest rate for seven months, as manufacturers passed on increases in input costs to their clients.

April data signalled that manufacturing employment edged higher, with a marginal increase in payroll numbers reported for the fourth successive month.

Where an increase in staffing was indicated, this was attributed to higher output and the introduction of new product lines.

However, some firms reported reducing headcounts due to weaker demand and through redundancy programs.

http://www.londonstockexchange.com/exchange/news/sharecast/news-detail.
html?newsId=20066612 (accessed 1 June 2011)

Glossary

Demand	الطلب	Exports	الصادرات
Index	مؤشر	Inflation	تضخم
Slowest rate	ابطأ معدل	Payroll	قائمة بأسماء العاملين
Manufacturing sector	قطاع التصنيع	Chief Executive	المدير التنفيذي

....
....
....
....
....
....
....
....
....
....
....
....
....
....
....
....
....
....
....
....
....

LESSON 18: TERMINOLOGY: ACCOUNTING AND AUDIT

Accounting and audit translations include various documents such as financial statements (accounts statements, balances, memos, memoirs, treasury reports, budget and variance reports, audit reports, accounting software, accounting standards and international accounting standards), in addition to articles on accounting and accounting books.

> *18.1 Identify the title, the introduction, the responsibilities of directors and auditors, the basis of opinion of the auditors, the opinion of the auditors, the signatures of the auditors, and the date of the following report.*

Independent Auditors' Report

To The Shareholders of XXX Bank

Report on the Financial Statements
We have audited the accompanying consolidated financial statements of your Corporation and its subsidiaries [together 'the group'] which comprise the consolidated statement of financial position as at 31 december 2013 and the consolidated statements of income, comprehensive income, cash flows and changes in equity for the year then ended, and a summary of significant accounting policies and other explanatory information.

Board of Directors' Responsibility for the Financial Statements
The board of directors is responsible for the preparation and fair presentation of these consolidated financial statements in accordance with international financial reporting Standards, and for such internal control as the board of directors determines is necessary to enable the preparation of the financial statements that are free from material misstatement, whether due to fraud or error.

Auditors' Responsibility
Our responsibility is to express an opinion on these consolidated financial statements based on our audit. We conducted our audit in accordance with international Standards on auditing. Those standards require that we comply with ethical requirements and plan and perform the audit to obtain reasonable assurance about whether the consolidated financial statements are free from material misstatement.

An audit involves performing procedures to obtain audit evidence about the amounts and disclosures in the financial statements.

The procedures selected depend on the auditors' judgement, including the assessment of the risks of material misstatement of the financial statements, whether due to fraud or error. In making those risk assessments, the auditors consider internal control relevant to the entity's preparation and fair presentation of the financial statements in order to design audit procedures that are appropriate in the circumstances, but not for the purpose of expressing an opinion on the effectiveness of the entity's internal control.

An audit also includes evaluating the appropriateness of accounting policies used and the reasonableness of accounting estimates made by the board of directors, as well as evaluating the overall presentation of the financial statements.

http://www.etisalat.com/en/system/docs/reports/Q4-2012-Interim-Financial-Report.pdf (accessed 14 April 2013)

....

....

....

....

....

....

18.2   Translate the previous audit report. Make sure you follow the conventional pattern of auditor's reports.

....

....

....

....

....

....

....

....

....

....

....

....

....

....

....

....

....

....

....

....

....

....

....

....

....

....

....

....

....

....

....

....

....

....

....

....

....

18.3 Make a list of the new economic terms you could translate into Arabic in the following introduction to an article on the economic crisis. The first paragraph is translated as an example.

Introduction
Andy Kilmister

There are three important starting points for understanding the current economic crisis. Firstly, what is happening at the moment represents the break-up of the interlocking set of arrangements by which the world economy has been governed since the mid-1980s.

These arrangements represented a temporary 'solution' for capital to the crises which emerged a decade earlier. Secondly, the crises of the 1970s and the attempts to resolve them of the 1980s arose from a central contradiction within capitalism between the creation of profits in the sphere of production and the realisation of those profits in the sphere of circulation and exchange. Thirdly, the historically weak situation of British capital, at least that section of British capital territorially located in Britain, has left Britain especially vulnerable to the crisis.

Arabic translation

في البداية هنالك ثلاث نقاط مهمة لفهم الأزمة الاقتصادية الراهنة. أولا، إن ما يحدث حاليا يمثل تفكك سلسلة الترتيبات المتداخلة التي تحكم الاقتصاد العالمي منذ أواسط الثمانينات حيث شكلت تلك الترتيبات حلولا مؤقتة للأزمة التي ظهرت من عقد مضى . ثانيا، نبعت أزمات السبعينات والمحاولات لحلها في الثمانينات من التناقض الرئيس في الرأسمالية بين تحقيق الأرباح في مجال الإنتاج، ونتائج تلك الأرباح في مجال التوزيع والتبادل. ثالثا، أصبحت بريطانيا عرضة لهذه الأزمة التي سببتها حالة الضعف التي عانى منها الاقتصاد البريطاني، وعلى الأقل ذلك الجزء من رأس المال الموجود في بريطانيا.

The crisis itself has a number of dimensions but three in particular are crucial. The first is the build-up of debt, both corporate and household debt, but especially household debt. Linked with this is the likelihood of a return to international monetary instability and of the refusal of the rest of the world to fund US (and UK) trade deficits. The third factor is the effect of the ecological crisis on the world economy, which brings with it the prospect of an end to two decades of low commodity prices. However, these should be seen as medium-term developments, determining the underlying tensions within which more immediate changes take place.

A Marxist analysis of the crisis needs to be based on an analysis which can grasp these underlying structural factors, see how these play themselves out in surface phenomena and also understand the competing strategies of capital as it attempts to manage the crisis.

http://www.internationalviewpoint.org/spip.php?article1581 (accessed 28 May 2011)

....

....

....

....

....

....

....

....

....

....

....

....

....

....

....

 18.4 *Now translate the rest of the article. Pay attention to the cohesive devices and grammatical structures.*

Recession and the Financial Crisis

The most important current development in the wake of the banking crisis is the transmission of that crisis to the rest of the economy and its interaction with the more general economic crisis now emerging. The most obvious issue here is the onset of recession. The central reason for the recession is the dependence of consumer demand in particular but also business investment on high levels of debt over the last two decades. Now that lending is contracting this debt-fuelled expansion is no longer possible and a sharp economic slowdown looks inevitable. The fall in house prices is also worsening the slowdown in consumer spending as households can no longer borrow against rising equity values.

There are two fundamental reasons for the reliance on debt. Consumption has come to depend on debt because of the contradiction between driving wages down to generate profits in production and needing to ensure demand in order to sell the goods produced and realise these profits. The most obvious manifestation of this is growing income inequality and it is no accident that the build-up of debt has been worst in countries with the greatest disparity in incomes, notably the UK and USA.

Linked to this is the way in which production in general, but especially investment, has come to rely on debt as a result of the weakness of profitability in the productive sector. As Robert Wade puts it 'the rate of profit of non-financial corporation's fell steeply between 1950–73 and 2000–06 – in the US, by roughly a quarter. In response firms "invested" increasingly in financial speculation'. Consequently, without debt being available to fund expansion recession appears inevitable.

http://www.internationalviewpoint.org/spip.php?article1581 (accessed 28 May 2011)

Glossary

Dimensions	أبعاد	**Competing strategies**	استراتيجيات منافسة
Economic crisis	أزمة إقتصادية	**Recession**	ركود
Interlocking	متداخلة	**Consumer demand**	طلب المستهلك
Capitalism	الرأسمالية	**Investment**	الاستثمار
Debt	دين	**Interest rates**	معدلات الفائدة
Instability	عدم استقرار		

....

....

....

....

....

....

....

....

....

....

....

....

....

....

....

....

....

....

....

1. *Translate the following extracts into Arabic.*

How to Brand a Next-Generation Product
Carmen Nobel

When Apple launched its latest iPad, experts and nonexperts alike expected it to be dubbed 'iPad 3', a natural follow-on to the second-generation iPad 2. Instead, the company called the new iPad just that: 'the new iPad'. Observers debated whether this was lazy branding or a very deliberate effort to market the iPad as a sibling to the Mac. Macs keep their names with each successive upgrade, analysts noted, while iPhones sport sequential numbers and letters to indicate improvements.

....
....
....
....
....

'Consumers don't necessarily read specs to learn about new features, but they'll always notice a new name.'
Like Apple, most consumer-centric companies deal with the dilemma of how to brand the next-generation of an existing product. Product upgrades make up the majority of corporate research and development activity. That's why Harvard Business School marketing professors John T. Gourville and Elie Ofek were surprised to find a dearth of academic research on the subject. 'There's a lot of research about new-product branding, but as best as we could tell, nobody had looked closely at the issue of how to brand a successive generation,' Gourville says.

....
....
....
....
....
....

....

....

....

....

....

....

Brand name continuation vs. name change

In one experiment, 78 participants considered a hypothetical scenario in which a well-known firm is preparing to launch a new version of its colour printer. The participants, who were split into two groups, received a list of seven successive model names. For the first group, the entire series of printers was branded in a sequential fashion, from 2300W to 2900W. For the second group, the first four models were named sequentially – 2300W to 2600W, but the last three models reflected a brand name change – MagiColor, MagiColor II, and MagiColor III.

Based on the names alone, on a scale of 1 to 7, participants gauged the likelihood of significant changes and improvements for each successive model. Even though participants had no information about the actual features of the products, participants predicted much greater change when the latest version was named MagiColor than when it was named 2700W.

http://hbswk.hbs.edu/item/6961.html (accessed 29 May 2011)

....

....

....

....

....

....

....

....

2. *Translate the following business letter into Arabic.*

Subject: Confirmation of Balance as of 31 July 2012

Dear Mr Smith,

With reference to above noted subject, please note that we are in the process of reconciling our records with our account for audit of our financial statements. In connection therewith, kindly confirm the balance due to/from us on account as at Date 30-06-2012

Please state in the space below whether or not this is in agreement with your records as the above date. Please furnish the information you may have that will assist us in reconciling the differences.

An early response shall be highly appreciated.

Yours sincerely

http://www.learningall.com/2012/05/customer-balance-confirmation-letter-sample
(accessed 14 April 2013)

....

....

....

....

....

....

....

....

....

....

....

....

3. *Translate the following into Arabic.*

The balance sheet is a snapshot of a company's –

- assets (what it owns)
- liabilities (what it owes)
- owners' equity (net worth – what's left over for the owners)

The balance sheet snapshot is at a particular point in time, such as at the close of business on December 31. The simplest corporate balance sheet possible, showing only totals and leaving out all detail, might look like this

ALBEGA CORPORATION Balance Sheet December 31, 20xx				
Assets	$485,000	Liabilities		$285,000
		Shareholders' Equity		$200,000
Total Assets	$485,000	Total Liabilities and Shareholders' Equity		$485,000

Balance sheet equation. Assets are always equal to the liabilities plus equity. You can see the balance sheet as a statement of what the company owns (assets) and the persons having claims to the assets (creditors and owners). Here is the balance sheet equation:

Assets = Liabilities + Shareholders' Equity	
Assets	Liabilities
	Shareholders' Equity

The equation reflects how information is organized on the balance sheet, with assets listed on the left and liabilities and equity on the right. Like the equation, the two sides of the balance sheet must balance.

http://users.wfu.edu/palmitar/Law&Valuation/chapter%203/3-2-1.htm (accessed 15 April 2013)

....

....

....

....

....

....

....

....

....

....

....

....

....

....

....

....

....

....

 4. *Translate the following text on international accounting standards (IAS). Follow the strategies discussed earlier when translating abbreviations and acronyms. Make a list of abbreviations and their translations.*

IAS 1 Presentation of Financial Statements as issued at 1 January 2009

This extract has been prepared by IASC Foundation staff and has not been approved by the IASB. For the requirements reference must be made to International Financial Reporting Standard. This Standard prescribes the basis for presentation of general purpose financial statements to ensure comparability both with the entity's financial statements of previous periods and with the financial statements of other entities. It sets out overall requirements for the presentation of financial statements, guidelines for their structure and minimum requirements for their content.

A complete set of financial statements comprises:

a) a statement of financial position as at the end of the period;
b) a statement of comprehensive income for the period;
c) a statement of changes in equity for the period;
d) a statement of cash flows for the period;
e) notes, comprising a summary of significant accounting policies and other explanatory information; and
f) a statement of financial position as at the beginning of the earliest comparative period when an entity applies an accounting policy retrospectively or makes a retrospective restatement of items in its financial statements, or when it reclassifies items in its financial statements.

http://www.iasb.org/NR/rdonlyres/9DC65C49-ABA2-4718-954A-49775B5C84E6/0/IAS1.pdf (accessed 2 June 2011)

Glossary

Financial statements	كشف الحساب	Comprehensive income	الدخل الشامل
Standard	معيار	Equity	حقوق الملكية
Comprises	يتألف من	Retrospectively	بأثر رجعي

....

....

....

....

....

....

....

....

....

....

....

....

....

....

5. *Translate the following extracts taken from an economics web page.*

Britain has become, once more, a high-inflation economy. Normally as a nation we like to top any European league. But when that league is for inflation rates across Europe, that is more than a little embarrassing.

New Eurostat figures, which the Labour party was quick to pick up on, show that last month Britain had the highest inflation rate in the European Union. Yes, of all 28 EU members states, Britain's inflation rate was the highest.

http://www.economicsuk.com/blog/001944.html (accessed 28 October 2013)

....

....

....

....

....

....

....

6.   *Discuss the features of a text with the class and the problems you encountered in translating it.*

Scientific Texts

Scientific texts are considered the most challenging for the translator. The term 'science' covers a wide range of disciplines that could include, but are not limited to, physics, biology, chemistry, astronomy, mathematics, geology, biochemistry, astrophysics, ecology and engineering sciences. Scientific texts differ from other texts basically because 'scientific language draws on humanistic education, while workshop terms are non-literary, practical, colloquial and sometimes humorous' (Pinchuk 1977: 167). Scientific texts are 'set out and presented in unqualifiedly objective terms for the reader of SL and TL text alike' (Bassnett-McGuire 1991b: 79). They are more challenging, for example than literary texts, especially because 'if the text is perceived as an object that should only produce a single invariant reading, any "deviation" on the part of the reader/translator will be judged as transgression' (ibid.).

Part of the difficulty in translating such texts arises from their use of specialised terminology: a large number of very specific terms and concepts, as well as numbers, symbols, graphs and diagrams. This can be challenging for the translator who does not have sufficient knowledge of these fields. Indeed, exceptional language and writing skills are required to enable the translator to transmit technical content in one language into another in a clear and precise manner. Furthermore, translators have to keep themselves completely up to date with the continuous changes in scientific terminology, neologisms and new technological advances.

However, many of these new terms used in scientific texts might not have a direct translation in the TL. If the text contains a lot of unknown terms, or terms coined for the first time, a common strategy is for translators to leave the term in the original language and apply a footnote to fully explain it in the TL. In some cases there may be fairly extensive glossaries of terms in the original text. Again, this poses a particular challenge to the scientific translator. But providing a faithful translation of a glossary of terms is likely to be a very difficult task since there are no dictionary equivalents for many of the terms being used.

LESSON 19: TRANSLATION STRATEGIES

The translator of scientific texts needs to choose the most appropriate strategy that facilitates the accurate transfer of the message from the SL to the TL. Though the easiest is not necessary the most appropriate, it could function as a first step towards finding the strategy that works. This section reviews some strategies employed in translating scientific texts.

1. Borrowing

This strategy involves introducing the SL term into the TL, and it is done in the following three ways:

- Total borrowing, where a full phonological borrowing of the terms takes place. For instance, *computer* is translated as كمبيوتر. Such borrowing accepts derivation so the word *computers* is translated as كمبيوترات. This strategy works best for new scientific terms that have no equivalents in the TL, new inventions, new diseases or scientific discoveries. It is usually referred to as *Arabisation*.
- Loan translations or *calque*, which involves providing a translation of the new term in TL. For example, *atomic number* is translated as العدد الذري and *atomic mass* as الكتلة الذرية.
- Naturalisation, where the SL term is adapted to the morphology of the TL. This strategy is common with the terminology of computer sciences and technology, chemistry and biology. Examples:
  - face books (plural) فيسبوكات /faisbūkāt/
  - To face book: يفسبك /yufasbik/
  - computers كمبيوترات/kumbiyūtarāt/
  - e-mails: إيميلات /īmaylāt/
  - faxes: فاكسات/fāksāt/.

2. Coinage

With this strategy new terms are created in the TL. The following are the three basic strategies for coinage in Arabic (Baker 1987: 186–7):

1. Derivation: according to this process, Arabic derives new terms by analogy based on its derivation system. Nominal and verbal forms are derived from the trilateral root. Derivation is considered 'the most natural way of enriching the language without altering its identity' (ibid.). For example, *data* is translated as معطيات (givens), taken from أعطى (give).
2. Al-istinbāṭ (discovery): involves the revival of old words by extending their meanings to express new concepts, e.g. *cloning* is translated as استنساخ.
3. Loan translations: the meaning of the term is translated literally into Arabic. For example, *electronic e-mail* is translated as البريد الإلكتروني .

Other solutions suggested by scholars for the problem of technical terms as well as other difficult words in the SL tackle the lack of lexical correspondence between the ST and TT at the word level, above word level, and textual equivalence: coping with cohesion and coherence. These problems will be discussed below with various suggestions for translation methods to deal with these issues.

19.1 *Read the following text, then complete the exercises that follow.*

How to Send Email Attachments

Email attachments allow you to send files along with your email messages. An attachment can be any type of file, but the most common ones are text *documents* and *images* (photos etc).

Before you send an attachment, you need to know where it is located on your computer. Usually you will have saved the file using Windows Explorer or some other software. Whenever you save a file to use as an attachment, select '*Save As ...*' and make a note of where you save it. If you can't find a file, use the *Windows search function*.

Once you know where the file is you can create the email message.

- Create a new *email message* and enter the usual details (recipient address, subject, etc).
- Look for an icon in your *toolbar* which looks like a paper clip and click it.
- A 'Browse' window will open. Locate and select the attachment file.

The file will now be attached to the email. Send the email in the normal way.

Important: before you send an attachment, you must be sure the person receiving it will be able to open it. Not all attachments will work on someone else's computer!

In order to open your attachment the recipient must have the appropriate software. Some types of files are very common and most people can open them, but other types can be rare or require expensive software.

These files are quite common and safe.

http://www.mediacollege.com/internet/email/attachments.html (accessed 17 March 2012)

19.2 *Apply* Arabisation *or* loan translation *to the italicised words.*

Arabisation	Loan translation

19.3 Read the following text and its translation and find examples of naturalisation, Arabisation and coinage.

Chemical Reactions

A reaction between an acid and a base to form a salt and water as the only products.

Hydrochloric acid and sodium hydroxide → sodium chloride and water

$$HCl + NaOH \rightarrow NaCl + H_2O$$

Sulphuric acid and potassium hydroxide à potassium sulphate and water

$$H_2SO_4 + 2KOH \rightarrow K_2SO_4 + 2H_2O$$

Nitric acid and calcium hydroxide à calcium nitrate and water

$$2HNO_3 + Ca(OH)_2 \rightarrow Ca(NO_3)_2 + 2H_2O$$

http://www.sky-web.net/science/reaction-types.htm#acidbase (accessed 11 February 2012)

Arabic translation

لإنتاج الملح والماء كمركبات، تتفاعل الأحماض والقواعد.

حامض الهيدروكلوريك وهيدروكسيد الصوديوم ← كلوريد الصوديوم وماء

$$HCl + NaOH \rightarrow NaCl + H_2O$$

حامض الكبريتيك وهيروكسيد البوتاسيوم ← سلفات البوتاسيوم والماء

$$H_2SO_4 + 2KOH \rightarrow K_2SO_4 + 2H_2O$$

حامض النتريك وهيروكسيد الكالسيوم ← نترات الكالسيوم والماء

Arabisation	Loan translation

19.4 *Translate the following paragraph into English.*

تتكون الأحماض النووية DNA و RNA من سلاسل من وحدات كيميائية تسمى بـ النيكلوتيدات، ويتكون كل نيوكلوتيد من ثلاث مكونات رئيسية:

• (جزيء سكر خماسي) رايبوز، أو رايبوز منقوص الأكسجين. (مجموعة من الفوسفات)
• قاعدة نيتروجينية. وتتكون القواعد النيتروجينية من:

أ- بيورينات، وتشمل قاعدتين هما: أدنين A، غوانين G، وتتألف كل منها من حلقتين.

ب- بيرمدينات، وتشتمل على ثلاث قواعد: ثايمين T، سايتوسين C، ويوراسيل U، ويتألف كل منها على حلقة واحدة.

و يختلف تركيب النيوكليوتيدات بعضها عن بعض بناء على نوع القاعدة النيتروجينية الموجودة فيها، وجزيء السكر.

http://ar.wikipedia.org/wiki/حمض نووي (accessed 5 August 2013)

....

....

....

....

....

....

....

LESSON 20: TRANSLATION PROBLEMS AND PRACTICAL STEPS

Accuracy is a major issue to be taken into consideration when translating scientific texts. The translator should make sure that the translation conveys the same objectives of the SL, thus contributing to the major scientific areas introduced in the SL. Proficiency in the TL is not sufficient since translators need to know the language of the discipline they are dealing with, as well as its jargon and historical background, so that they can articulate their ideas competently in the TL following the content and the style of the ST. Scientific translation is sometimes viewed as a *communicative service*, which offers new information for a new audience; its basic goal is to deliver scientific information that may be used *easily, properly and effectively* (Byrne 2006: 10). If certain terminology in the original text requires more elaboration in the TL, the translator must ensure that this extended explanation (e.g. added in a footnote) remains within the grasp of the reader. For this purpose, the scientific translator should be a good researcher to keep up with all new development, since scientific discoveries evolve very rapidly.

The first step involves understanding the scientific content of the article so that a conceptual map of the original text is created. This process involves analysing the text on two levels, lexical and grammatical. Lexical analysis involves looking up the technical terms, using a good technical dictionary, and identifying the text's register. Grammatical analysis involves a contrastive analysis of grammatical structures in the SL and TL. In the case of translating from English into Arabic, there are many differences as far as the grammar of both languages is concerned. English is characterised by a scarcity of connectives, little repetition of keywords, extensive use of passive forms, and the verbs *to be* and *to have*. Arabic, on the other hand, uses more connectives, repeats key words more often and favours active structures. Tense and aspect are also problematic in both languages.

20.1 *Read the following text, then complete the activities that follow.*

Dual Therapy with Aliskiren plus ACE Inhibitor or ARB Is Linked to Hyperkalemia

Risk was about 50% higher with dual therapy than with monotherapy.

Angiotensin-converting–enzyme (ACE) inhibitors and angiotensin-receptor blockers (ARBs) block different steps of the renin-angiotensin system. Aliskiren (Tekturna) directly inhibits renin (the first step of the renin-angiotensin system) and is approved for treatment of hypertension. Although seemingly attractive, dual therapy with ACE inhibitors and ARBs is associated with elevated risks for acute kidney injury and hyperkalemia. Whether the same is true for dual therapy with aliskiren plus an ACE inhibitor or an ARB is unclear.

In this meta-analysis of 10 randomized controlled trials involving more than 4800 people, risk for hyperkalemia was significantly higher among patients receiving dual

94

therapy with aliskiren plus an ACE inhibitor or an ARB than among patients receiving monotherapy with an ACE inhibitor or an ARB (relative risk, 1.6; number needed to harm, 43) or aliskiren (RR, 1.7; number needed to harm, 50). Risk for acute kidney injury was not higher among patients receiving dual therapy with aliskiren plus an ACE inhibitor or an ARB than among patients receiving monotherapy with an ACE inhibitor, ARB, or aliskiren.

Comment: Dual therapy with aliskiren and an ACE inhibitor or an ARB is associated with excess risk for hyperkalemia. Notably, the Aliskiren Trial in Type 2 Diabetes using Cardio-Renal Endpoints (ALTITUDE) was recently terminated because patients randomized to aliskiren plus an ACE inhibitor or an ARB experienced elevated risk for adverse events including hyperkalemia, 'renal complications,' and nonfatal stroke (Novartis media release Dec 20 2011). Clinicians should not prescribe aliskiren in combination with an ACE inhibitor or an ARB.

— Paul S. Mueller, MD, MPH, FACP
Published in *Journal Watch General Medicine*, 9 February 2012.

http://general-medicine.jwatch.org/cgi/content/full (accessed 8 February 2012)

20.2 *Identify the basic technical terms and provide English into Arabic translation of these terms.*

Term	Translation

20.3   Identify the passive structures and decide how they should be rendered in Arabic.

SL passive	TL structure

20.4   Translate the first two paragraphs into Arabic.

....

....

....

....

....

....

....

....

....

....

....

....

....

....

....

....

....

20.5   Read the following text then translate it into English using the most appropriate tense.

يرتبط مرض السكري بهرمون الانسولين الذي تفرزه البنكرياس حيث يسبب نقص افراز هذا الهرمون مرض السكري حيث يزيد السكر في الدم ولا يستطيع الجسم الاستفادة منه ولذلك يظهر في الدم. وهناك نوعين من السكري وهو سكري الاطفال والسكري الذي يصيب البالغين.

....

....

....

....

....

....

LESSON 21: TRANSLATION PROBLEMS: MORE PRACTICE

Arabic is a highly inflected language compared to English which uses very few inflections. Arabic has inflections for tense, number and gender. Furthermore, while English has inflection for plural only, Arabic has inflections for singular, dual and plural. For example, English uses the pronoun 'it' to refer to both the electron and the atom while Arabic treats the electron as masculine and the atom as feminine. This grammatical gender distinction is shown in the inflections of the verbs that follow these nouns. For instance, if you want to translate the sentence 'the proton is located in the centre of the atom', you should treat the proton as masculine saying:

يقع البروتون في مركز الذرة.

The word 'atoms' in the sentence 'Atoms are the smallest particle into which an element can be divided.' is treated as feminine plural and therefore the verb is inflected with feminine inflection at the beginning:

الذرات أصغر الجزيئات التي يمكن أن تقسم لها العناصر

21.1 Read the following text and answer the questions below before you translate it.

Atoms and Molecules

Most of the Universe consists of matter and energy. Energy is the capacity to do work. Matter has mass and occupies space. All matter is composed of basic elements that cannot be broken down to substances with different chemical or physical properties. Elements are substances consisting of one type of atom, for example Carbon atoms make up diamond, and also graphite. Pure (24K) gold is composed of only one type of atom, gold atoms. Atoms are the smallest particle into which an element can be divided. The ancient Greek philosophers developed the concept of the atom, although they considered it the fundamental particle that could not be broken down. Since the work of Enrico Fermi and his colleagues, we now know that the atom is divisible, often releasing tremendous energies as in nuclear explosions or (in a controlled fashion in) thermonuclear power plants.

Subatomic particles were discovered during the 1800s. For our purposes we will concentrate only on three of them, summarized in Table 1. The proton is located in the centre (or nucleus) of an atom, each atom has at least one proton. Protons have a charge of +1, and a mass of approximately 1 atomic mass unit (amu). Elements differ from each other in the number of protons they have, e.g. Hydrogen has 1 proton; Helium has 2.

The neutron also is located in the atomic nucleus (except in Hydrogen). The neutron has no charge, and a mass of slightly over 1 amu. Some scientists propose the neutron is made up of a proton and electron-like particle.

The electron is a very small particle located outside the nucleus. Because they move at speeds near the speed of light the precise location of electrons is hard to pin down. Electrons occupy orbitals or areas where they have a high statistical probability of occurring. The charge on an electron is –1. Its mass is negligible (approximately 1800 electrons are needed to equal the mass of one proton).

http://www.emc.maricopa.edu/faculty/farabee/biobk/biobookchem1.html   (accessed 8 February 2012)

Glossary

Matter	مادة	Atomic mass	الوزن الذري
Energy	طاقة	Nucleus	النواة
Elements	عناصر	Electron	الكترون
Atom	ذرة	Particle	جزيء

21.2 Identify the verbs to be *and* to have *in the text and decide how to translate them.*

....

....

....

....

....

....

....

....

....

21.3 Underline the passive sentences in the text above and choose the most appropriate tense when translating them into Arabic.

....

....

....

....

....

....

....

....

....

....

....

....

....

....

....

Notice that Arabic does not have an equivalent perfective aspect or verb *to be* used as in English. These are not normally translated into Arabic. For example, the following sentence is usually translated as follows:

Elements are substances consisting of one type of atom.

العناصر مواد تتألف من نوع واحد من الذرات.

As you can see, the verb 'are' is not translated into Arabic.

21.4 *Find similar examples in the previous text and provide their Arabic translation.*

....

....

....

....

....

....

....

....

....

LESSON 22: PROBLEMS OF WORD LEVEL EQUIVALENCE

Problems with finding the right scientific equivalents are basically related to the types of words used. The following types of words require special care in translation (Baker 1992/2006: 21–6).

- Culture-specific concepts
- The SL concept is not lexicalised in the TL
- The SL word is semantically complex
- The SL and TL make different distinctions in meaning
- The TL lacks a superordinate
- The TL lacks a specific term (hyponym)
- Differences in physical or interpersonal perspective
- Differences in the expressive meaning
- Differences in form
- Differences in frequency and purpose of using specific forms
- The use of loan words in the ST

The following strategies could be followed to deal with these items.

- Translation by a more general word (superordinate)
- Translation by a more neutral/less expressive word
- Translation by cultural substitution
- Translation using a loan word or loan word plus explanation
- Translation by paraphrase using a related word
- Translation by paraphrase using unrelated words
- Translation by omission
- Translation by illustration (Baker 1992/2006: 26–42)

22.1   Read the following text and identify the problems related to the lack of a superordinate or a specific term (hyponym) in the TL, and to the differences in physical or interpersonal perspective. Then suggest the most appropriate strategies before you provide your translation. Complete the table below.

Etiology

Sources

Coronaviruses (CoVs) are found in a wide range of animal species, including in cats, dogs, pigs, rabbits, cattle, mice, rats, chickens, pheasants, turkeys, and whales, as well as in humans. They cause numerous veterinary diseases (e.g. feline infectious peritonitis, avian infectious bronchitis); they can also cause upper and, more commonly, lower respiratory tract illness in humans (group 1 [human CoV 229E] and group 2 [human CoV OC43]).

The near absence of SARS-CoV antibodies in persons who did not have SARS demonstrated that SARS-CoV had not circulated to any significant extent in humans before 2003 and was introduced into humans from animals. Preliminary data after the outbreak started suggested that animals in the markets of Guangdong province in China may have been the source of human infection. However SARS-CoV like viruses were not found in animals prior to arrival in the markets.

A wide range of other coronaviruses in bats has been found, suggesting that bats are the most likely animal reservoir for the SARS outbreak. SARS infection in animals before arrival in the markets was uncommon, and these animals were probably not the original reservoir of the outbreak, although they may have acted as amplifying hosts. The proximity in which humans and livestock live in rural southern China may have led to the transmission of the virus to humans.

http://emedicine.medscape.com/article/237755-overview (accessed 17 March 2012)

Glossary

Etiology	علم اسباب الامراض	Transmission	نقل
Peritonitis	التهاب الصفاق	Amplifying	مضخم
Antibodies	اجسام مضادة	Hosts	مضيف
Respiratory	تنفسي		

Strategies	Problems	Examples

22.2   *Provide your translation here.*

....

....

....

....

....

....

....

....

....

....

....

....

....

....

....

....

....

....

....

....

....

22.3   *Read the following text, identify translation problems and choose the most appropriate strategy to account for each of them. Complete the table below.*

Pathophysiology

The lungs and gastrointestinal tract have been demonstrated to be the only major organ systems that support SARS-CoV replication.

After establishment of infection, SARS-CoV causes tissue damage by (1) direct lytic effects on host cells and (2) indirect consequences resulting from the host immune response. Autopsies demonstrated changes that were confined mostly to pulmonary tissue, where diffuse alveolar damage was the most prominent feature.

Pathologic slide of pulmonary tissue infected with severe acute respiratory syndrome–associated coronavirus. Diffuse alveolar damage is seen along with a multinucleated giant cell with no conspicuous viral inclusions. Courtesy of the US Centers for Disease Control and Prevention.

Multinucleated syncytial giant cells were thought to be characteristic of SARS but were rarely seen. Angiotensin-converting enzyme-2 (ACE-2), being a negative regulator of the local rennin-angiotensin system, was thought to be a major contributor to the development of this damage.

The other mechanism was thought to be the induction of apoptosis. The SARS-CoV–3a and –7a proteins have been demonstrated to be inducers of apoptosis in various cell lines.

Immunologically, SARS is characterized by a phase of cytokine storm, with various chemokines and cytokines being elevated.

http://emedicine.medscape.com/article/237755-overview#a0104 (accessed 17 March 2012)

 Glossary

Gastro	معدي	Immunologically	مناعيا
Infection	عدوى	Multinucleated	متعدد النوى
Apoptosis	الموت الخلوي المبرمج	Major contributor	عامل اساسي
Coronavirus	الفيروس المكلل	Inducers	محرضات

Strategies	Problems	Examples

22.4 *Provide your own translation of the above text.*

....

....

....

....

....

....

....

....

....

....

....

....

....

....

....

....

....

....

....

22.5 *Read the following texts. Then choose two problems that were not tackled in the previous exercises, comment on them and provide the most appropriate strategies to follow. Complete the table below. After translating the texts, exchange your work with another student and comment on each other's translation and discuss.*

Cellular binding

Single-stranded ribonucleic acid (RNA) viruses such as the SARS-CoV have no inherent proofreading mechanism during replication. Accordingly, mutations in the RNA sequence replication of coronaviruses are relatively common. Such mutations can cause the resulting new virus to be either less or more virulent.

The surface envelop S protein of SARS-CoV is thought to be a major determinant in establishing infection and cell and tissue tropism. This protein, after binding to its receptor – which is thought to be angiotensin-converting enzyme 2 (ACE-2) and is expressed in a variety of tissues, including pulmonary, intestinal, and renal – undergoes conformational change and cathepsin L–mediated proteolysis within the endosome.

The binding of SARS-CoV to DC-SIGN (dendritic cell-specific intercellular adhesion molecule-grabbing nonintegrin), which recognizes a variety of microorganisms, does not lead to entry of the virus into dendritic cells. It instead facilitates the transfer and dissemination within the infected host.

Immune response

The type I interferon (IFN-alfa/beta) system represents a powerful part of the innate immune system and has potent antiviral activity. However, SARS-CoV discourages attack by the IFN system. Replication of the virus occurs in cytoplasmic compartments surrounded by a double membrane layer. Such concealment within cells probably causes a spatial separation of the viral pathogen-associated molecular patterns (PAMPs) and the cellular cytoplasmic pattern recognition receptors (PRRs).

In addition, the activation of IFN regulatory factor–3 (IRF-3) is actively inhibited by SARS-CoV, with IRF-3 being targeted by 5 known SARS-CoV proteins in order to prevent IFN-system activation. IFN induction can also be affected by unspecific degradation of host messenger RNA (mRNA).

These defensive measures prevent tissue cells from mounting an antiviral IFN attack following SARS-CoV infection. Ultimately, however, an IFN immune response can occur. Plasmacytoid dendritic cells (PDCs) use Toll-like receptors (TLRs) to recognize pathogen structures and use IRF-7 to induce IFN transcription. Large amounts of IFN are thus produced by the PDCs following infection with SARS-CoV.

http://emedicine.medscape.com/article/237755-overview#aw2aab6b2b3 (accessed 20 March 2012)

Epidemiology

In November 2002, an unusual epidemic of severe pneumonia of unknown origin in Guangdong Province in southern China was noted. There was a high rate of transmission to health care workers (HCWs). Some of these patients were positive for SARS-CoV in the nasopharyngeal aspirates (NPA), whereas 87% patients had positive antibodies to SARS-CoV in their convalescent sera. Genetic analysis showed that the SARS-CoV isolates from Guangzhou had the same origin as those in other countries, with a phylogenetic pathway that matched the spread of SARS to other parts of the world.

The 2002–2003 SARS outbreak predominantly affected mainland China, Hong Kong, Singapore, and Taiwan. In Canada, a significant outbreak occurred in the area around Toronto, Ontario. In the United States, 8 individuals contracted laboratory-confirmed SARS. All patients had travelled to areas where active SARS-CoV transmission had been documented.

SARS is thought to be transmitted primarily via close person-to-person contact, through droplet transmission. Most cases have involved persons who lived with or cared for a person with SARS or who had exposure to contaminated secretions from a patient with SARS. Some affected patients may have acquired SARS-CoV infection after their skin, respiratory system, or mucous membranes came into contact with infectious droplets propelled into the air by a coughing or sneezing patient with SARS.

Leaky, backed-up sewage pipes; fans; and a faulty ventilation system were likely responsible for a severe outbreak of SARS in the Amoy Gardens residential complex in Hong Kong. Transmission may have occurred within the complex via airborne, virus-laden aerosols.

The worldwide number of SARS cases from the original outbreak (November 2002 through July 31, 2003) reached more than 8000 persons, including 1706 healthcare workers. Of those cases, 774 resulted in death, with a case fatality ratio of 9.6% deaths, and 7295 recoveries.

http://emedicine.medscape.com/article/237755-overview#a0156 (accessed 20 March 2012)

Glossary

Tropism	انتحاء	Contaminated	ملوث
Immune response	الاستجابة المناعية	Secretions	افرازات
Epidemiology	علم الاوبئة	Mucous membrane	الغشاء المخاطي
Pneumonia	التهاب رئوي		

Strategies	Problems	Examples

22.6 *Provide your translation here.*

LESSON 23: PROBLEMS ABOVE WORD LEVEL EQUIVALENCE

These problems are related to collocation, idioms and fixed expressions (Baker 1992: 46–77). For collocations, the following problems were identified:

- The engrossing effect of ST patterning
- Misinterpreting the meaning of SL collocation
- The tension between accuracy and naturalness
- Culture-specific collocations
- Marked collocations in the ST

The solutions suggested by Baker include the following steps:

- Take the effect of SL into consideration
- Put the translation draft aside for a few hours and return to read the target text so that the possible interfering influence of source text patterning is reduced
- Evaluate the significance of a potential change in meaning
- Translation by a marked collocation depending on the constraints of the target language and the purpose of the translation

For idioms and fixed expressions, the following problems are identified:

- Recognition
- No equivalent in the TL
- A similar counterpart in the TL with a different context of use
- An idiom used in the ST both in its literal and idiomatic sense at the same time
- Difference between the convention, context and frequency of use in the SL and TL

The suggested methods include:

- Resourcing
- Using an idiom of similar meaning and form
- Using an idiom of similar meaning but differing form
- Paraphrase
- Omission
- Compensation
- Rewording
- Translation by paraphrase using unrelated words
- Translation by illustration

23.1 Identify problems above word level related to the collocations in the text below and determine the strategies to be followed in translating them. Complete the table below.

Prognosis

WHO data indicate that mortality from SARS is highly variable. The mortality rate has been found to range from less than 1% in patients below age 24 years to more than 50% in patients aged 65 and older. Certain risk factors, including the following, have been associated with a poorer prognosis:

- Older age
- Chronic hepatitis B infection
- Laboratory features - Including marked lymphopenia and leukocytosis, elevated lactate dehydrogenase level, hepatitis, high SARS-CoV viral load, and comorbidities such as diabetes mellitus.

Elevated levels of interferon-inducible protein 10 (IP-10), monokine induced by IFN-gamma (MIG), and interleukin 8 (IL-8) during the first week, as well as an increase of MIG during the second week, have also been associated with a poor prognosis.

A study of SARS survivors found that most of these had significant improvement clinically, radiographically, and in their pulmonary function studies. However, 27.8% of patients still exhibited abnormal radiographs at 12 months. Significant reductions in the diffusing capacity of carbon monoxide and in exercise ability (6-min walking distance) were also documented at 12 months. Polyneuropathy and myopathy associated with critical illness, avascular necrosis (possibly steroid induced), steroid toxicity, and psychosis were some of the other long-term sequel observed in the SARS survivors.

Morbidity and mortality

SARS can result in significant illness and medical complications that require hospitalization, intensive care treatment, and mechanical ventilation.

Morbidity and mortality rates were observed to be greater in elderly patients. The overall mortality rate of SARS has been approximately 10%. According to the CDC and WHO, the death rate among individuals older than age 65 years exceeds 50%.

http://emedicine.medscape.com/article/237755-overview#aw2aab6b2b5 (accessed 20 March 2012)

 Glossary

Mortality	معدل الوفيات	Morbidity	نسبة انتشار المرض
Chronic	مزمن	Myopathy	التهاب العضلات
Hepatitis	التهاب الكبد	Necrosis	موت الانسجة
Comorbidities	الامراض المصاحبة	Psychosis	اضطراب عقلي
Toxicity	سمية		

Strategies	Problems	Examples

23.2   Provide your translation here.

....

....

....

....

....

....

....

....

....

....

....

....

....

....

....

....

....

....

....

....

....

....

....

....

23.3 *Identify problems and strategies related to the translation of idioms and fixed expressions in the following text before providing a full translation. Complete the table below.*

Alzheimer's disease: Your Role as Caregiver

Do You Realize How Much You Do?
Your role as caregiver to a loved one suffering from Alzheimer's disease can be very involved.

- You help maintain the quality of life for your spouse, parent, family member, or friend with Alzheimer's disease.
- You have become educated about symptoms, treatments and the progression of the disease.
- You probably keep track of appointments with the doctor, medication schedules, and exercise.
- You offer the love and support necessary to meet the challenges of Alzheimer's disease.

You are a caregiver. While many patients retain their independence for a period of time after being diagnosed with Alzheimer's disease, some may need more help with performing daily activities. For others, the diagnosis may come after weeks or months of you coping with symptoms that did not have a name. Regardless of how long you've been dealing with Alzheimer's disease or to what degree, in some way Alzheimer's has affected your life and responsibilities – physically, emotionally, or economically.

Recommended Related to Alzheimer's

Alzheimer's disease Diagnosis
Unfortunately, getting an Alzheimer's disease diagnosis is not simple. Your doctor can't check for the disease by doing a quick blood test. That's because signs of Alzheimer's disease do not appear in your blood. Instead, Alzheimer's disease is the result of a problem inside your brain. The only way to be 100% certain a person suffers from Alzheimer's disease is to examine samples of brain tissue. This can only be done during an autopsy, after a person has died.

Read the Alzheimer's disease Diagnosis article
The role you have taken on is not an easy one. However, the following tips offer some guidance on how to maintain and improve your caregiving relationship:

- **Take time for yourself.** Make sure you have time to relax. If necessary, enlist the help of other family members or even hire someone to help out.
- **Learn as much as you can about your loved one's disease** so you will know how you can help. You'll also understand what changes to expect in your loved one's behavior or symptoms.

http://www.webmd.com/alzheimers/guide/role-caregiver (accessed 20 March 2012)

Glossary

Symptoms	اعراض	**Consult**	يستشير
Diagnosed	مشخص	**Caregiving**	تقديم الرعاية
Autopsy	تشريح		

Strategies	Problems	Examples

23.4 *Provide your translation here.*

....

....

....

....

....

....

....

....

....

....

....

....

....

....

LESSON 24: TEXTUAL EQUIVALENCE: COHESION AND COHERENCE

Cohesion and coherence are two main aspects of discourse. Coherence is defined as 'a tacit, but discernible, thematic or emotional development running through the text' (Dickins 2005: 128) as shown by the following example:

> I was hungry. I went downstairs. I knew the kitchen was on the ground floor. I was pretty sure the kitchen was on the ground floor. I didn't expect to find it easily. I made myself a sandwich. (Ibid. p. 135)

The Arabic version is:

> لقد كنت جائعا. ذهبت إلى الطابق الأرضي. كنت أعرف أن المطبخ كان بالطابق الأرضي. كنت متأكدا بأن المطبخ كان بالطابق الأرضي لم أتوقع أن أجده بسهولة. أعددت لنفسي شطيرة.

According to Dickins, although the above text lacks cohesive markers to link the sentences, it is nonetheless coherent as a result of the chronological narrative structures.

The following problems and strategies are related to maintaining cohesion and coherence between the SL and TL:

1. The tension between word order and communicative function.
    Suggested strategies: voice change, change of the verb, nominalisation, and extraposition.
2. Maintaining a balance between accuracy and naturalness as far as the cohesion of the text is concerned.
    Suggested strategies: gender adding, person deleting, verb tense reordering, restrictions of word order, producing different lexical chains, change of meaning explicitation according to word order deictic, rechunking (reorganising or renumbering paragraphs, sentences), and text-type repunctuating (Baker 1992: 166–215).

24.1 *Read the following text and provide a cohesive translation. Then carry out a contrastive analysis of the SL and TL as far as the cohesive devices are concerned.*

Cardiac enzyme studies measure the levels of the enzyme creatine phosphokinase (CPK, CK) and the protein troponin (TnI, TnT) in the blood. Low levels of these enzymes and proteins are normally found in your blood, but if your heart muscle is injured, such as from a heart attack, the enzymes and proteins leak out of damaged heart muscle cells, and their levels in the bloodstream rise.

Because some of these enzymes and proteins are also found in other body tissues, their levels in the blood may rise when those other tissues are damaged. Cardiac enzyme studies must always be compared with your symptoms, your physical examination findings, and electrocardiogram (EKG, ECG) results.

Why It Is Done
Cardiac enzyme studies are done to:

- Determine whether you are having a heart attack or a threatened heart attack (unstable angina) if you have chest pain, shortness of breath, nausea, sweating, and abnormal electrocardiography results.
- Check for injury to the heart after bypass surgery.
- Determine if a procedure, such as percutaneous coronary intervention (PCI), or a medicine to dissolve the blockage (thrombolytic medicine) has successfully restored blood flow through a blocked coronary artery.

How to Prepare
No special preparation is required before having this test.

Many medicines may affect the results of this test. Be sure to tell your health professional about all the nonprescription and prescription medicines you take.

Talk to your doctor about any concerns you have regarding the need for the test, its risks, how it will be done, or what the results will mean. To help you understand the importance of this test, fill out the medical test information form.

How It Is Done
The health professional drawing your blood will:

- Wrap an elastic band around your upper arm to stop the flow of blood. This makes the veins below the band larger so it is easier to inject a needle into the vein.
- Clean the needle site with alcohol.
- Put the needle into the vein. More than one needle stick may be needed.
- Attach a tube to the needle to fill it with blood.
- Remove the band from your arm when enough blood is collected.
- Put a gauze pad or cotton ball over the needle site as the needle is removed.
- Put pressure on the site and then put on a bandage.

http://www.webmd.com/heart-disease/cardiac-enzyme-studies (accessed 24 January 2012)

Cohesive devices in SL	Cohesive devices in TL	Examples

24.2 *Provide your own translation of the above text.*

....

....

....

....

....

....

....

....

....

....

....

....

....

....

....

....

....

....

....

....

....

....

....

....

....

....

....

24.3 *Provide your own translation of the following text taking into consideration the differences in the use of the cohesive devices.*

من الأسباب التي تستدعي إجراء عملية زراعة القلب الإصابة بالقصور القلبي الذي يعرف ب "بالقصور القلبي الاحتقاني" أيضاً، وتحدث عندما لا يتمكن القلب من ضخ الكمية الكافية من الدم الذي يحمل الأكسجين إلى أعضاء الجسم المختلفة، بحيث يستمر القلب في عملية الضخ إلا أنها ليست بنفس فعالية القلب السليم. فيحتفظ جسم الإنسان المصاب بالقصور القلبي الاحتقاني بكمية أكبر من السوائل مما تؤدي إلى انتفاخ الكاحلين والساقين، كما و تتجمع السوائل في الرئتين مسببة ضيق في التنفس.

http://www.kfshrc.edu.sa/wps/portal/!ut/p/c0/04 (accessed 6 August 2013)

....

....

....

....

....

....

....

....

....

....

....

....

....

....

....

....

....

....

....

....

MODULE REVIEW EXERCISES

1. *Read the following article carefully and do the exercises that follow. The first paragraph has been translated as an example.*

DNA AND MOLECULAR GENETICS the physical carrier of inheritance

While the period from the early 1900s to World War II has been considered the 'golden age' of genetics, scientists still had not determined that DNA, and not protein, was the hereditary material. However, during this time a great many genetic discoveries were made and the link between genetics and evolution was made.

الـ د ن أ (DNA) والجين الجزيئي الناقل العضوي للوراثة

في حين اعتبرت الفترة من 1900 وحتى الحرب العالمية الثانية العصر الذهبي لعلم الجينات فإن العلم لم يكن قد حسم أمره في أن الـ د ن أ (DNA) هو مادة الوراثة وليس البروتين. ورغم ذلك فقد شهدت هذه الفترة عدة اكتشافات جينية وتم الربط بين الجينات والنشوء.

Friedrich Meischer in 1869 isolated DNA from fish sperm and the pus of open wounds. Since it came from nuclei, Meischer named this new chemical, nuclein. Subsequently the name was changed to nucleic acid and lastly to deoxyribonucleic acid (DNA). Robert Feulgen, in 1914, discovered that fuchsin dye stained DNA. DNA was then found in the nucleus of all eukaryotic cells.

During the 1920s, biochemist P.A. Levene analyzed the components of the DNA molecule. He found it contained four nitrogenous bases: cytosine, thymine, adenine, and guanine; deoxyribose sugar; and a phosphate group. He concluded that the basic unit (nucleotide) was composed of a base attached to a sugar and that the phosphate also attached to the sugar. He (unfortunately) also erroneously concluded that the proportions of bases were equal and that there was a tetranucleotide that was the repeating structure of the molecule. The nucleotide, however, remains as the fundamental unit (monomer) of the nucleic acid polymer. There are four nucleotides: those with cytosine (C), those with guanine (G), those with adenine (A), and those with thymine (T).

During the early 1900s, the study of genetics began in earnest: the link between Mendel's work and that of cell biologists resulted in the chromosomal theory of inheritance; Garrod proposed the link between genes and "inborn errors of metabolism"; and the question was formed: what is a gene? The answer came from the study of a deadly infectious disease: pneumonia. During the 1920s Frederick Griffith studied the difference between a disease-causing strain of the pneumonia causing bacteria (*Streptococcus peumoniae*) and a strain that did not cause pneumonia. The pneumonia-causing strain (the S strain) was surrounded by a capsule.

http://www.emc.maricopa.edu/faculty/farabee/biobk/biobookdnamolgen.html (accessed 12 March 2012)

2. *Provide Arabic equivalents for the following terms.*

English	Arabic
DNA	
Nucleotide	
Adenine	
Guanine	
Deoxyribose sugar	
Thymine	
Cytosine	

3. *Translate the third and fourth paragraphs of the above text. Use a specialised dictionary.*

....
....
....
....
....
....
....
....
....
....
....
....
....
....
....
....
....
....

....

....

....

....

....

....

 4. Translate the following text, bearing in mind gender and number differences between English and Arabic.

The atomic number is the number of protons an atom has. It is characteristic and unique for each element. The atomic mass (also referred to as the atomic weight) is the number of protons and neutrons in an atom. Atoms of an element that have differing numbers of neutrons (but a constant atomic number) are termed isotopes. Isotopes can be used to determine the diet of ancient peoples by determining proportions of isotopes in mummified or fossilized human tissues. Biochemical pathways can be deciphered by using isotopic tracers. The age of fossils and artefacts can be determined by using radioactive isotopes, either directly on the fossil (if it is young enough) or on the rocks that surround the fossil (for older fossils like dinosaurs). Isotopes are also the source of radiation used in medical diagnostic and treatment procedures.

www.emc.maricopa.edu/faculty/farabee/biobk/BioBookCHEM1.html (accessed 8 February 2012)

Glossary

Atomic number	الرقم الجزيئي	Radioactive	مشع
Atomic mass	الكتلة الذرية	Diagnostic	تشخيصي

....

....

....

....

....

....

....

....

....

....

....

....

....

....

5. *Translate the following excerpt and make a glossary of the scientific terms.*

Most heart attacks are the end result of coronary heart disease, a condition that clogs coronary arteries with fatty, calcified plaques. As blood flow is gradually impeded, the body may compensate by growing a network of collateral arteries to circumvent blockages; the presence of collateral vessels may greatly reduce the amount of heart muscle damaged by a heart attack. In the early 1980s, researchers confirmed that the precipitating cause of nearly all heart attacks is not the obstructive plaque itself, but the sudden formation of a blood clot on top of plaque that cuts off blood flow in an already narrowed vessel.

http://www.webmd.com/heart-disease/guide/heart-attack-causes-treatments (accessed 25 October 2013)

....

....

....

....

....

6. *Translate the following scientific terms from Arabic into English using a specialised dictionary.*

1. عملية التمثيل الضوئي. ....

2. انقسام الخلية. ....

3. النظرية النسبية. ....

4. المركبات الكيميائية . ...

5. التفاضل والتكامل في الرياضيات. ....

Media Texts

Media texts deal with the main means for receiving information and entertainment, the language usually found in articles and advertisements published in newspapers or broadcast on radio, TV, websites, etc. These depend on the addressee and their main function is to express the message in an effective way, so they emphasise the layout and mode of presentation. In newspapers, for example, the message is aided with much focus on the display of headlines/banners (font size, organisation, prominence and other typographical features) in the way most appealing to readers.

Being a sub-category of non-fiction, media texts do not always apply the literary use of language. First, media texts tend to adopt a different structure. Careful structuring is important for all types of text, 'whether you're writing a novel, a letter to a friend, or a recipe, clear structuring is the key of effective communication' (Rowland and Avery 2001: 111). Indeed, structuring of texts is vital not only for strengthening one's argument, but for the coherent flow of information. However, unlike conventional writing, media texts often have a different opening and emphasis. While literary texts, for example, habitually offer a clear introduction, media texts open with what is often referred to as a 'lead' which is used to 'create suspense or surprise, or shock or arouse emotions in the reader' (ibid. p. 112).

Moreover, the language of media texts is characterised by being more free than standard language. The media style, unlike the literary, is often geared towards the production of news and information in a very limited timeframe. The nature of news production necessitates a simple style, with very short sentences and subtle cohesive devices that are almost absent. On the sentence and paragraph level, therefore, sentences and paragraphs are short and economical, and on the grammatical level, the use of active rather than passive verbs is preferred and the presence of adjectives is limited (Garcia Suares 2005; Hernandez Guerrero 2005, quoted in Bielsa 2009: 147–8). Especially when the language is attention-grabbing (e.g. a headline), it tends to be free from grammatical constraints. For example, a newspaper headline would read, 'State population to double by 2040; babies to blame.' instead of a more grammatical sentence such as 'The state population is expected to double by 2040 and babies are the ones to blame.' It is clear how short the headline is, omitting functional words and focusing only on the meaningful lexis. According to Reah (2002: 13), 'the headline has a range of functions that specifically dictate its shape, content and structure, and operates within a range of restrictions that limit the freedom of the writer'. These restrictions are indicated in the condensed heading or title that is often used for marketing purposes, and with the intention of attracting the reader. To this end, 'headline writers use a wide range of devices to create a very specific style, which is sometimes called headlines' (Verdonk 2002: 4).

Internally also, media language is less elaborate than other types. In Arabic, for instance, media sentences are less complex, with the main function of conveying information away from the creative stylistic aspects of the text. Rhetorical and aesthetic features are minimised, with more emphasis on plain language to convey the meaning. The elaborate cohesive devices that are the ingredients of the Arabic writing style are less common in media texts. Sentences and paragraphs are often connected by the conjunctive device *wa* (and). However, because it aims to grab attention, media language tends to make more use of emotive language, although this depends on the type and category of media texts. This variation in style is heavily often influenced by the pressing need to publish information, in some cases instantly, but sometimes with emphasis on the creative aspects of writing so as to appeal to readers' emotions in a piece of news.

Media texts can be divided into four categories: hard news, feature articles, special-topic news and headlines. These categories have different features, depending on the theme and structure of the text. Some of the texts are written very quickly, with the sole aim of publishing and disseminating news and information, often on the same day (Bell 1991: 14). They may take many forms, for example, 'an interview with a person in the news or an eyewitness to a press release from a public relations agency, a government media briefing, a copy from an international news agency such as Reuter's or United Press International' (Rowland and Avery 2001: 121). Such varieties will normally differ in form and language.

Different kinds of media also have their own characteristics depending on their purpose. Magazine covers, for example, have less text and no advertising, compared to newspapers. In a newspaper, for instance, there are usually different sections for sports, entertainment, a TV guide, medical and scientific news, etc. each with its own genre-specific language (ibid.). Each of these sub-categories of media language has different features, all of which serve the purpose of creating expressive and informative texts.

With regard to the translation profession, media texts require more interpreting than written translation. Interpreting is usually more complicated and difficult to tackle than written translation because of difficulties regarding the setting, time, voice, participants, etc. As for written translation, media texts can be more easily translated than other complex genres such as literary texts. In translating lexis for example, the translation strategies used are restricted to using a borrowed term, being either transliterated or translated literally. This is especially true because these terms tend to be restricted in meaning and cannot normally be used in other connotative senses such as metaphor or metonymy. For example, media terms such as *Piggyback* have straightforward equivalents in other languages, e.g. *ferroutage* in French and *huckepack* in German. This characteristic makes media texts a successful candidate for machine translation programs. Such programs can be more and more refined and much appreciated since the language of the media can be anticipated, similar to other 'technical' language uses. Indeed, media texts could be called a category of technical texts if we consider the media as a 'field' and not strictly a discipline. What follows is a wide range of drills designed to help learners and translators to practise translating media texts, taking into account some of the translation strategies introduced in the previous modules.

LESSON 25: CONFLICTS/CIVIL WARS

Translating texts about conflicts and wars remains one of the most complex tasks faced by translators. This is due to the fact that the type of register used may be interpreted differently by different parties involved in the conflict. For example, what could be considered as a 'holy war' by some could be regarded as a 'guerrilla war' by others. These ideological differences in the way terms are approached and actions are labelled make it difficult for translators to provide a representative translation for certain terms and actions. In this case, the translator needs to take into account different aspects (i.e. cultural, social and political) of the TT and ST, meaning that the translator should be very aware of these cultural differences in order to provide a balanced translation. In translating what could be deemed as controversial terminologies, the translator could resort to footnotes to explain or contextualise these key terms in the SL, so that the TL audience is aware of the main aspects underlining these terminologies in the source text.

25.1   *Identify the main media features in the text below.*

Traumatised Syrians flee to Jordan

There is mounting pressure on the Syrian government to suspend its attacks and allow humanitarian aid to enter the besieged towns of Homs, Deraa and Idlib. As government forces continue their bombardment of opposition held towns, thousands of Syrians have fled the fighting into neighbouring countries, including Jordan, from where Wyre Davies reports.

At a small, rather crowded primary school in the Jordanian border town of Ramtha, an English lesson is in progress.

It is no wonder some of the children look a bit bemused. The girls and boys in the front three rows are all from Syria.

A few weeks ago, they and their families were cowering in their homes, under fire from their own government's guns.

Now in the safety of neighbouring Jordan, some have been given places in local schools.

The latest shaky images from Syria show anti-government protests in several towns, despite the obvious dangers.

The assault on Homs, in particular, is relentless. Dozens of people have died in recent days.

At a house just across the plain from his troubled homeland, I met a former Syrian civil servant who fled the country with 10 members of his family when he was ordered to shoot protesters in Homs.

A loyal member of the Baath Party for more than 20 years, he was aghast that a regime he had served for so long was prepared to go to such lengths to quash the rebellion in Homs.

He asked me not to publish his name or exactly what his job was because, as he said, the Assad regime has a notorious network of informers and loyalists who keep close tabs on its opponents.

To his eternal regret, when the extended family left the besieged city – they had to leave behind two of their daughters, who have their own husbands and children to look after. They've not heard from them for more than a week.

Suspicious of authority

Jordan, of course, has a long history of hosting and accommodating refugee populations, from Palestinians to Iraqis.

Andrew Harper, a Middle East veteran, is the UNHCR's new representative in Jordan and is co-ordinating closely with the authorities in Amman to contain the crisis.

http://www.bbc.co.uk/news/world-middle-east-17151364 (accessed 24 February 2012)

Glossary

Mounting pressure	ضغوط متزايدة	**Anti-government protests**	الاحتجاجات المناهضة للحكومة
Suspend	وقف	**Close tabs**	بشكل وثيق
Humanitarian aid	المساعدات الإنسانية		
Bombardment	قصف	**Beseiged city**	المدينة المحاصرة
Cowering in their homes	يرتعدون في منازلهم	**Emphasise**	للتأكيد على
Shaky images	صور مهزوزة	**Avoiding some of the pitfalls**	وتجنب بعض العثرات
Assault	الهجوم		
Relentless	لا هوادة فيها		

25.2 *Summarise the above text in Arabic.*

....

....

....

....

....

....

....

....

....

....

....

....

....

....

....

....

....

....

....

25.3 *Translate the underlined words/phrases in the following extract into Arabic.*

There is mounting pressure on the Syrian government to <u>suspend</u> its attacks and allow humanitarian aid to enter the besieged towns of Homs, Deraa and Idlib. As <u>government forces</u> continue <u>their bombardment of opposition</u> held towns, thousands of Syrians have <u>fled the fighting</u> into neighbouring countries, including Jordan, from where Wyre Davies reports. At a small, rather <u>crowded primary school</u> in the Jordanian border town of Ramtha, an English lesson is in progress.

It is no wonder some of the children look <u>a bit bemused</u>. <u>The girls and boys in the front three rows are all from Syria.</u>

A few weeks ago, they and their families were cowering in their homes, under fire from their own <u>government's guns</u>. Now in the <u>safety of neighbouring</u> Jordan, some have been given places in local schools.

....

....

....

....

....

....

....

....

....

....

25.4 *Cross out the inaccuracies in the following Arabic translation of the English text below.*

Psychological effects

The shelling, the escape and the resettlement in Jordan have been deeply traumatic experiences, especially for the children.

'Psychologically it's affected them really badly,' one mother told me. 'They wouldn't leave my side because they were so scared and they were afraid of any noise.'

The town of Deraa, where the Syrian uprising against President Bashar al-Assad began and where there has been heavy fighting ever since, is clearly visible from the Jordanian side.

Aid agencies and many concerned governments are now pressing for the opening of humanitarian corridors to Deraa and other border towns.

Arabic translation

الآثار النفسية

وكانت عمليات الضرب، والهروب، وإعادة السكن في الأردن تجارب مؤلمة للغاية، وخاصة بالنسبة للأطفال.

وقالت أحد الأمهات "لقد أثرت نفسيا فيهم بشدة حقا". وأضافت "إنها لا تترك جانبي لأنها كانت خائفة جدا وكانوا خائفين من أي ضوضاء".

مدينة درعا، حيث الانتفاضة السورية ضد الرئيس بشار الأسد بدأ وحيث كان هناك قتال عنيف منذ ذلك الحين، واضحة تماما من الجانب الأردني.

وكالات الإغاثة وحكومات أخرى يضغطون الآن لفتح ممرات إنسانية إلى درعا وبلدات حدودية أخرى.

 25.5   *Translate the following Arabic text into English.*

   http://www.aljazeera.net/news/pages/72784666-df28-49d0-af3b-b0ff94912389

أعلن الائتلاف الوطني السوري المعارض أنه يسعى إلى جمع الفصائل المسلحة ضمن جيش موحد يسهل تمويله وتسليحه.

وقال عضو الائتلاف ميشال كيلو أمس في مقابلة أجريت معه في باريس إنه يتعين إعادة تنظيم الجيش الحر وهيكلته بقيادة حقيقية وانضباط, وأشار إلى رغبة الائتلاف في إنشاء مجلس تنفيذي من عشرة أعضاء يتولى إعادة التنظيم.

وأضاف أنه يجب إدماج الضباط السابقين الموجودين حاليا في الأردن وتركيا في الجيش الذي يعتزم الائتلاف الوطني بناءه. وتواجه كتائب الجيش الحر انتقادات في بعض المناطق التي تنتشر فيها بعدم انضباط بعض أفرادها وفشلها في تشكيل قوة موحدة تكون قادرة على مواجهة القوات الموالية للرئيس السوري بشار الأسد.

وفي المقابل, هناك فصائل مقاتلة إسلامية مثل كتائب أحرار الشام توصف بأنها الأكثر تنظيما وانضباطا, وهي في الغالب تعارض التنظيم تحت سلطة الائتلاف السوري المعارض.

وقال كيلو إن الائتلاف سيسعى إلى انتخاب المجلس التنفيذي المؤلف من عشرة أعضاء, الذي سيشرف على إعادة تنظيم الفصائل المسلحة, خلال اجتماع يعقد الشهر القادم.

وأضاف أن هذا المجلس سيكون بمثابة جهاز لخدمة السوريين في المناطق الخاضعة لسيطرة المعارضة, وتحدث عن نية الائتلاف إنشاء جهاز مالي للاستفادة من الأموال التي تحول من السوريين في الخارج, أو التي يمكن تحصيلها من الأنشطة الاقتصادية في المناطق الخارجة عن سيطرة النظام.

التسليح

ويشكل تسليح فصائل الجيش الحر المسألة الأكثر إلحاحا بالنسبة إلى الائتلاف الذي انتخب قبل أسابيع أحمد الجربا رئيسا جديدا له.

وقالت مصادر من الجيش الحر إنه بدأ يتلقى في الأيام الماضية أسلحة نوعية, خاصة منها المضادة للدروع. ولا تزال الدول الغربية تحجم عن إمداد المعارضة بالسلاح خشية أن تقع في أيدي فصائل توصف بالمتشددة.

وقال مسؤول أميركي أمس إن إدارة الرئيس باراك أوباما أحرزت تقدما باتجاه التغلب على المعارضة التي يبديها عدد من نواب الكونغرس لتسليح المعارضة السورية

(accessed 24 July 2013)

Lesson 26: Uprisings and revolutions

The 2011 uprisings and revolutions, which have engulfed the Middle East, have led to the coining of new terminologies and phrases that have become part of the Arabic glossary and culture, and which some translators might not be familiar with. Some of this new register is specific to individual countries and groups, and could pose a challenge to the translator. Translators, therefore, ought to be aware of the new register as well as the internal/local context associated with it, in order to be able to provide a representative and accurate translation of the meaning of the text. Another challenge when translating such texts is the culture-specific nature of some of this register. The historical context could prove essential, as some terms are directly linked to national and regional issues, which could be very specific to the context of the SL.

The following section will introduce learners and translators to some key terminologies related to uprising and revolutions. The range of drills offered will allow students to practise their translation skills.

26.1 *Identify the errors in the following Arabic translation of the English text below.*

---

http://www.guardian.co.uk/commentisfree/2011/feb/01/egypt-tunisia-revolt

> What cannot but strike the eye in the revolts in Tunisia and Egypt is the conspicuous absence of Muslim fundamentalism. In the best secular democratic tradition, people simply revolted against an oppressive regime, its corruption and poverty, and demanded freedom and economic hope. The cynical wisdom of western liberals, according to which, in Arab countries, genuine democratic sense is limited to narrow liberal elites while the vast majority can only be mobilised through religious fundamentalism or nationalism, has been proven wrong. The big question is what will happen next? Who will emerge as the political winner?
>
> When a new provisional government was nominated in Tunis, it excluded Islamists and the more radical left. The reaction of smug liberals was: good, they are basically the same; two totalitarian extremes – but are things as simple as that? Is the true long-term antagonism not precisely between Islamists and the left? Even if they are momentarily united against the regime, once they approach victory, their unity splits, they engage in a deadly fight, often more cruel than against the shared enemy.

(accessed 26 November 2012)

Arabic translation

من الممكن في ظل هذه الثورات الموجودة في تونس ومصر الغياب الواضح للإسلاميين، مادام وقد اعتاد الشعب في ظل التقليد الديمقراطي الإسلامي أن يثور ضد الحكام والفساد والفقر المرتبط بهم، والتقيد بمطالبات الحرية وآمال الاقتصادية. ولعل الحكمة التي يفتخر بها الليبراليون في الغرب، والتي تخرج من الفكرة القائلة بأن الحس الديمقراطي في الدول العربية مبني على النخبة الليبرالية وأن الأقلية الشعبية الكبيرة لا يتم تعليمها إلا من خلال القومية والأصولية الدينية، قد ثبت نجاحها. والسؤال الأهم الذي يطرح الآن " ما الذي سيحدث مستقبلاً؟ ومن الذي سيصعد ويبرز ليكون الفائز السياسي؟!

عندما تم تصويت الحكومة الانتقالية الجديدة في تونس، خرج منها الإسلاميون وجماعات اليسار الراديكالي، وكان رد فعل الليبراليين المعتدين بأنفسهم طيباً : فقد رأوا أنهم متشابهون إلى حد كبير، رغم التناقضات الكبيرة بينهم . ولكن هل تبدو الأشياء سهلة إلى هذا الحد؟! فهل تكون العداوة والخصومة طويلة المدى لم تعد بهذه الصفة وتلك الحدة بين الإسلاميين واليساريين؟ وحتى لو تسنى لهم أن يتحدوا معاً ضد النظام، فبمجرد اقترابهم من إحراز النصر، فإن هذه الوحدة ستنكسر، ما يولد لصراع دامي بينهم ربما يكون أشد شراسة وضراوة من هذا العداء المعلن ضد العدو المشترك.

26.2   Rewrite the following Arabic translation of the ST below in your own words without distorting the meaning.

---

http://www.guardian.co.uk/commentisfree/2011/feb/01/egypt-tunisia-revolt

And it is crucial to read the ongoing events in Tunisia and Egypt (and Yemen and … maybe, hopefully, even Saudi Arabia) against this background. If the situation is eventually stabilised so that the old regime survives but with some liberal cosmetic surgery, this will generate an insurmountable fundamentalist backlash. In order for the key liberal legacy to survive, liberals need the fraternal help of the radical left. Back to Egypt, the most shameful and dangerously opportunistic reaction was that of Tony Blair as reported on CNN: change is necessary, but it should be a stable change. Stable change in Egypt today can mean only a compromise with the Mubarak forces by way of slightly enlarging the ruling circle. This is why to talk about peaceful transition now is an obscenity: by squashing the opposition, Mubarak himself made this impossible. After Mubarak sent the army against the protesters, the choice became clear: either a cosmetic change in which something changes so that everything stays the same, or a true break.

(accessed 26 November 2012)

Arabic translation

تقتضي الضرورة الملحة في الوقت الحالي قراءة الأحداث الجارية في تونس ومصر (وربما تكون اليمن والمملكة العربية السعودية لاحقاً) في إطار هذه الخلفية التاريخية. فلو آل الوضع الراهن إلى الاستقرار في النهاية على أن يظل النظام القديم الحاكم قابضاً بزمام السلطة، ولكن مع بعض الإضافات الليبرالية التجميلية له، فإن هذا من شأنه أن يمهد لردة فعل أصولية لا يمكن أن تقهر. وحتى يظل هذا التراث الليبرالي قائماً، سيكون الليبراليون في أمس الحاجة إلى عون إخوانهم في اليسار الراديكالي. ولو نظرنا إلى مصر، لوجدنا أن أكثر ردود الفعل الانتهازية الخطيرة والمخزية تتبلور فيما قاله توني بلير لقناة الـ "سي إن إن" حين قال " التغيير ضروري، ولكن يجب أن يكون تغييراً متزناً. والتغيير المتزن المنشود الآن في مصر يمكن أن يفهم الآن على أنه بمثابة مساومة مع قوات مبارك أو التوصل لتسوية لتسوية ينبني على أساسها توسعة نطاق حكمه وسلطاته قبل أن تهتز. وهذا هو السبب بأن الحديث عن الانتقال السلمي للسلطة الآن يعتبر "عملا مشيناً"، حيث أن مبارك جعل، بتدميره وضعضعة للمعارضة، الأمر مستحيلاً. فبعد أن أمر مبارك بإرسال الجيش ضد المتظاهرين، كان الخيار واضحاً وجلياً: إما أن التغيير التجميلي، بمعنى أن تتغير الأشياء بشكل تظل في جوهرها على حالها، أو التغيير الحقيقي الشامل.

26.3   Read the following text and identify the major grammatical errors that have affected the Arabic translation.

http://www.theguardian.com/commentisfree/2011/feb/01/egypt-tunisia-revolt

The hypocrisy of western liberals is breathtaking: they publicly supported democracy, and now, when the people revolt against the tyrants on behalf of secular freedom and justice, not on behalf of religion, they are all deeply concerned. Why concern, why not joy that freedom is given a chance? Today, more than ever, Mao Zedong's old motto is pertinent: 'There is great chaos under heaven – the situation is excellent.'

Where, then, should Mubarak go? Here, the answer is also clear: to the Hague. If there is a leader who deserves to sit there, it is him.

(accessed 10 September 2013)

Arabic translation

وثمة قلق ليبرالي آخر تكمن في خوف من يقفز إحدى القوى السياسية المنظمة على السلطة بعد رحيل مبارك. والحقيقة أن أي من هذه المخاوف غير موجود، حيث أن مبارك أخذ ذلك بعين الاعتبار من خلال إبعاده لكافة أحزاب وحركات معارضة وجعلهم مهمشة حتى تكون النتيجة تشبه بعنوان رائعة أجاثا كريستي "وبعد ذلك كان لا شيء".

والآن، علينا نعرف أين تعين على مبارك أن يذهب بعد التنحي؟ وإليك بالإجابة الواضحة – إلى لاهاي، لأنه لو كان هناك زعيما يستحق الجلوس هناك، فهو مبارك من عليه ذلك.

26.4   Match the following sentences with their Arabic translations.

1. Carved into artificial states after the First World War, it's been bombed and occupied – by the US, Israel, Britain and France – and locked down with US bases and western-backed tyrannies.
2. But the fact that they kicked off against western-backed dictatorships meant they posed an immediate threat to the strategic order.
3. Sitting on top of the bulk of the globe's oil reserves, the Arab world has been the target of continual interference and intervention ever since it became formally independent.
4. As the Palestinian blogger Lina Al-Sharif tweeted on Armistice Day this year, the 'reason World War One isn't over yet is because we in the Middle East are still living the consequences'.
5. The Arab uprisings that erupted in Tunisia a year ago have focused on corruption, poverty and lack of freedom.

6. There's a real sense in which, more than any other part of the former colonial world, the Middle East has never been fully decolonised.

Arabic translation

1. هناك شعور حقيقي في الشرق الأوسط أكثر من أي بقعة أخرى من العالم الاستعماري سابقًا بأنَّ الشرق الأوسط لم يحصل على استقلاله بالكامل.

2. وكما كتبت المدونة الفلسطينية لينا الشريف على تويتر في يوم الهدنة في العام الحالي: "إنَّ السبب وراء عدم انتهاء الحرب العالمية الأولى حتى الآن، هو أننا في الشرق الأوسط ما زلنا نعيش عواقبها".

3. وبعد تقسيمه إلى دول صورية بعد الحرب العالمية الأولى، تم قصف واحتلال أجزاء منه بواسطة الولايات المتحدة الأمريكية وإسرائيل وبريطانيا وفرنسا كما تم محاصرته بالقواعد الأمريكية وأنظمة استبدادية مدعومة من الغرب.

4. وبسبب تربعه على عرش مخزون البترول الأكبر في العالم، تم استهداف العالم العربي بتدخلات وغزو مستمرين، حتى بعد حصوله رسميًا على الاستقلال.

5. ولكن حقيقة انطلاقهم ضد الديكتاتوريات المدعومة من الغرب تعني أنَّهم شكلوا تهديدًا فعليًا للنظام الإستراتيجي.

6. وقد ركزت الثورات العربية التي اشتعلت شرارتها الأولى في تونس العام الماضي على الفساد والفقر وانعدام الحريات.

26.5 *Replace the underlined words in the following Arabic translation with synonyms without distorting the meaning of the ST.*

---

http://www.guardian.co.uk/world/2011/feb/03/egypt-regime-death-toll-tahrir

> The Obama administration is working on a plan in which the Egyptian president, Hosni Mubarak, would stand down immediately in spite of claims yesterday he was intent on clinging on to power until the elections in the autumn.
>
> The White House, the state department and the Pentagon have been involved in discussions that include an option in which Mubarak would give way to a transitional government headed by the Egyptian vice-president, Omar Suleiman. Such a plan has the backing of the Egyptian military, the New York Times reported.
>
> Anti-government protesters are hoping they can force Mubarak from office today, a day they have dubbed 'departure Friday'. Fridays after midday prayers is traditionally an explosive point in Middle East countries, with masses taking to the streets after attendance at mosques.
>
> But Mubarak was defiant yesterday, insisting that he intended remaining in office until the autumn election. He said that while he was fed up after six decades of public service and wanted to leave, he feared that an early departure would lead to chaos.

(accessed 20 August 2012)

Arabic translation

تعمل إدارة الرئيس الأمريكي باراك أوباما جاهدة على إيجاد خطة لتنحي الرئيس المصري حسني مبارك الفوري عن السلطة، على الرغم من أن مبارك نفسه أعلن عن عدم تخليه على السلطة في مصر حتى موعد الانتخابات الرئاسية في الخريف القادم.

وكان البيت الأبيض قد دخل في نقاش مع وزارة الخارجية ووزارة الدفاع الأمريكية، وذلك لتحديد كيفية التعامل مع الموقف في مصر، حيث كانت إحدى الخيارات المتاحة تنحية مبارك وتولي نائبه عمرو سليمان المسئولية، ومن المرجح أن تحظى هذه الخطة بدعم الجيش المصري وفقا لما أكدته صحيفة نيويورك تايمز الأمريكية.

وكان المحتجون المعارضون للرئيس حسني مبارك يأملون أن يستطيعوا في النهاية إجباره على التنحي وترك الحكم، وذلك بعد أن أعلنوا أن تظاهراتهم التي خرجت الجمعة هي لحمل مبارك على الرحيل نهائيا عن الرئاسة وأطلقوا عليها "جمعة الرحيل"، والتي شهدت انفجار حشود المعارضين لمبارك في شوارع العديد من المدن المصرية بعد انتهاء صلاة الجمعة، لتخرج الجماهير من المساجد لتسيطر على الشوارع وتنادي برحيل مبارك عن الحكم.

لكن مبارك أعلن التحدي، وأكد الخميس الماضي على أنه يرغب في البقاء في سدة الحكم في مصر حتى الانتخابات الرئاسية القادمة والمقررة في الخريف، وأكد أنه بعد ما يزيد عن ستة عقود قضاها في خدمة مصر في مواقع متعددة يريد الرحيل بالفعل، لكنه يخشى من أن رحيله المبكر قد يتسبب في حدوث فوضى في البلاد.

LESSON 27: ELECTIONS AND OPPOSITIONS

Translating election texts and events is often considered straightforward, but in reality it can be a challenging process for those translators who have little or no knowledge of the target text culture, as some election terminologies may have different interpretations, depending on the context of the source text. The obvious strategy for dealing with such texts is to have a good acquaintance with current affairs, as well as with registers related to elections and oppositions. In Arabic, different groups and opposition parties are given different labels and attributions, which could be confusing for translators who might not be aware of these political differences.

A glossary of these terminologies, therefore, as well as a good knowledge of current affairs could help translators overcome some of the challenges related to translating this register.

 27.1 Translate the following text employing the strategy of adaptation (see Lesson 5). Then provide antonyms in Arabic for the underlined words and phrases.

http://www.aljazeera.com/news/europe/2012/03/201234174822513879.html

Putin, who has dominated Russian politics since the <u>beginning of the 21st</u> century, won almost 64 per cent of votes, Russia's Central Election Commission said.

'According to <u>the preliminary</u> results, Vladimir Vladimirovich Putin has been elected president of the Russian Federation,' the head of the election commission Vladimir Churov told reporters on Monday.

Addressing tens of thousands of <u>supporters</u> in Moscow late on Sunday, a <u>tearful</u> Putin said the Russian people had <u>clearly rejected</u> the attempts of unidentified enemies to 'destroy Russia's statehood and usurp power'.

'The Russian people have shown today that such scenarios <u>will not succeed</u> in our land,' said Putin, flanked by outgoing President Dmitry Medvedev. 'They shall not pass!'

'I promised you we would win. We have won. <u>Glory</u> to Russia. We <u>won in an open</u> and fair struggle.'

But the scale of Putin's victory was questioned by some of his <u>rivals, and opposition activists</u>, who called for protests on Monday over allegations of <u>vote-rigging</u>.

(accessed 10 March 2012)

....

....

....

....

....

....

....

....

....

....

....

....

....

....

27.2   Read the following text and translate the underlined words and phrases into Arabic. Then compare and contrast the cohesive devices employed in the ST and TT.

http://www.theguardian.com/commentisfree/2011/feb/01/egypt-tunisia-revolt

Even in the case of clearly <u>fundamentalist movements</u>, one should be careful not to miss the <u>social component</u>. The Taliban is regularly presented as a fundamentalist Islamist group enforcing its rule with <u>terror</u>. However, when, in the spring of 2009, they took over the Swat valley in Pakistan, the *New York Times* reported that they engineered 'a class revolt that exploits <u>profound fissures</u> between a small group of <u>wealthy landlords</u> and their <u>landless tenants</u>'. If, by 'taking advantage' of <u>the farmers' plight</u>, the Taliban are creating, in the words of the *New York Times*, 'alarm about the risks to Pakistan, which remains largely <u>feudal</u>,' what prevented <u>liberal democrats</u> in Pakistan and the US similarly '<u>taking advantage</u>' <u>of this plight</u> and trying to help the landless farmers? Is it that <u>the feudal forces</u> in Pakistan are the natural ally of liberal democracy?

The inevitable conclusion to be drawn is that the rise of <u>radical Islamism</u> was always the other side of the disappearance of <u>the secular left</u> in Muslim countries. When Afghanistan is portrayed as the utmost <u>Islamic fundamentalist country</u>, who still remembers that, 40 years ago, it was a country with a strong <u>secular tradition</u>, including a <u>powerful communist party</u> that took power there independently of the Soviet Union? Where did this secular tradition go?

(accessed 10 September 2013)

....

....

....

....

....

....

....

....

....

....

....

....

....

....

....

....

....

....

27.3 *Extract three main headings in Arabic from the following text.*

http://www.guardian.co.uk/commentisfree/2011/nov/30/egypt-victor-election-democracy

There are international and regional forces that seek to restore the policies and personalities of the defunct regime. They realise that the Arab people will regain their independence – and a greater political, cultural and economic unity – if the Arab spring is completed. To these forces we say: the differences of opinion between the political parties will only produce increased co-operation for the greater good of our country; and the stability of Egypt, its transition to democracy and building of a democratic society in tandem with other Arab states, especially in north Africa, will have positive effects on the Mediterranean basin, Europe and the world.

We have a deep trust in all sections of Egyptian society and their determination to rebuild their country, and restore its leadership role in this region. We look to the future with hope. Egyptians will continue to make history.

(accessed 2 December 2011)

1. ....

2. ....

3. ....

27.4 *Remove any unnecessary information in the Arabic translation of the following English text.*

Our great revolutionary youth, who started and are still guarding the revolution, must also bear their solemn responsibility before the country and history. The handover of the power to the people in a peaceful manner through the ballot box is the safest and quickest way of ensuring the return of the armed forces to their natural role. We all want to build a new police force imbued with a new culture: one that respects the citizens and their rights, protects them when they express their opinions, and dares not to attack them.

Arabic translation

وعلى الشباب العاقل الثائر والغاضب، الذي وبكل صدق وإخلاص بدا الثورة وحماها، أن يتحمل مسئوليته كاملة وبدون شك أمام الله والوطن والتاريخ، وأن يدرك أن تسليم السلطة المؤقت للشعب بسلاسة عبر صناديق الاقتراع هو أسلم وأقصر الطرق للخروج من عنق الزجاجة الضيق وإعادة القوات المسلحة إلى دورها الطبيعي والدستوري ، وأننا جميعاً متفقون كليا على تسليم السلطة للشعب ليختار بإرادته الحرة من يحكمه ، وإننا جميعا نريد بناء جهاز شرطة جديد بثقافة أخرى جديدة وسلوكيات تحترم المواطن المتضامن وحقوقه وتحميه أثناء تعبيره عن رأيه ولا يجرؤ على الإعتداء عليه .

27.5 *Based on the following ST, fill in the blanks in the Arabic text below with the appropriate translation.*

http://www.theguardian.com/commentisfree/2012/feb/06/syria-massacres-hama

As for the supposed weakness and organisational ability of the Syrian opposition, there is in fact a huge capacity to organise and instil discipline. The people's co-ordinating committees administer to the people's needs efficiently. They communicate between themselves in all parts of Syria, assigning duties and dealing with logistics in a manner that is now much better than it was in the early days of the revolution. At the same time, the Syrian National Council has begun to organise its ranks abroad, agreeing on a political discourse that is more coherent and co-ordinated. True, the Syrian opposition is less well organised than their counterparts in Egypt, Tunisia and Yemen because of the extreme brutality of the Syrian regime, but an acceptable measure of maturity and commitment has been achieved. The street, with its civil and political forces, is able to guide the process of transition to democracy with no less proficiency than the other peoples in the region who have already got rid of their regimes.

(accessed 25 November 2013)

Arabic translation

أما المخاوف من ضعف .... فالواقع يدل على أن هناك ....
.... قد تشكل بالفعل في الداخل، فلجان التنسيق الشعبي تدير ....، وتتواصل فيما
بينها في مختلف أنحاء سوريا، وتوزع مهام .... بشكل أفضل بكثير مما كان علي الحال في
الأيام الأولى، في الوقت الذي بدأ المجلس الوطني الانتقالي ينظم هو الآخر ....، ويتفق على
خطاب سياسي أكثر .... صحيح أن المعارضة السورية .... من مثيلاتها
في مصر وتونس واليمن بسبب .... النظام السوري، ولكن الواقع يثبت أن قدرا مقبولا من
.... قد تحقق، وأن الشارع بقواه .... قادر على إدارة الانتقال إلى ....
.... لا تقل عن بقية الشعوب التي أطاحت بنظمها. .... التي شهدتها
سوريا في جمعة (عذرا حماة سامحينا) تدل على أن الشعب السوري قد حسم .... باتجاه
إسقاط النظام، وعلى المجتمع الدولي لا سيما روسيا والصين، أن يطلب .... هو الآخر من حماة ومن
حمص وإدلب ومن عموم الشعب السوري وأن ....، فللشعب هذه المرة صوت مسموع
وصورة متداولة كما أن له ذاكرة لا تموت.

27.6 *Indirectly report the following direct speech into Arabic.*

Salwa Muhanna, a retired administrative secretary, said: 'I'm very excited, I've never done anything like this before. Of course it's not perfect, but this is the kind of step forward for our country that I've dreamed of all my life. It's a historic moment for us and for the region, and no one can take that away.

'I voted for [liberal] Amr Hamzawy as he is young and we need a new generation of politicians to solve this country's problems. We must resist the threat of the Salafists and the Brotherhood.'

....

....

....

....

....

....

....

....

As with previous genres, translating this type of text requires a good knowledge of both the ST and TT cultural contexts, since some of the texts could be influenced by cultural and religious beliefs, which could be received differently by different audiences. The Arabic culture is religious oriented, and this is often evident in texts about natural disasters, since most Arabs and Muslim believe that disasters are an act of God. This may not be the case for other cultures, however, and therefore the translator should exercise extra caution while attempting to convey the meaning of the source text to the target audience. An awareness of the recipients' cultural beliefs and values is vital. The Arabic style in this genre of texts can be very informative, while also employing religious and sentimental lexis.

28.1 Read the following text and answer the questions below in Arabic.

20,000 dead in earthquake in Pakistan

The death toll in Pakistan and the Pakistani-controlled Kashmir province has now reached at least 20,000, in addition to hundreds killed in India and Afghanistan, due to an earthquake that hit the region on Saturday. Tens of thousands of those affected by the earthquake in the mountainous areas of northern Pakistan have spent their second night without shelter.

The survivors in several remote villages are still without shelter, medicine, food supplies and clean water. Amjad Anwar, an elderly inhabitant of the village of Patal, near Balakot, said: 'We don't want helicopters hovering over us. All we want is blankets and water.'

The epicentre was 80km northeast of Pakistan's capital, Islamabad. India and Afghanistan were also hit by the quake, which reached 7.6 on the Richter scale, making it the strongest earthquake in the region for nearly 100 years.

The epicentre of the earthquake was close to the city of Muzaffarabad, capital of the Pakistani-controlled Kashmir province. BBC correspondent Nick Bryant reported from Muzaffarabad, that the situation in the city, where numerous buildings have been destroyed, is dire. The cricket stadium in the city is being used to shelter the homeless, and provide aid to the survivors and the injured while they wait to be airlifted to hospitals in Islamabad.

Child Victims
Pakistani officials said that the north-west frontier was the worst-affected by the earthquake, as well as the Pakistani-controlled Kashmir province. The press reported that more than 400 children were killed when two schools collapsed in the north-west frontier. The Indian interior ministry said that many villages were flattened in the earthquake, and more than 600 people were killed.

The BBC's correspondent in Sirinjar reported that the local government is currently working on reinstating basic services, such as electricity and water.

Glossary

The number of casualities reached	بلغ عدد القتلى	Victims of Flood	ضحايا فيضانات
Earthquake	الزلزال	Survivors	الناجون
Affected by disaster	المنكوبين	Stranded	محاصر
Shelter (n)	مأوى	Livestock	الماشية
Survivors	الناجون	Provide aid to the survivors	توفير الإغاثة للناجين
Remote	النائية	Disaster	الكارثة
Shelter the homeless	إيواء المشردين	Embark on digging	انكب على الحفر
Provide aid to the survivors	توفير الإغاثة للناجين	Strong flood	فيضانات عارمة
Under the debris	تحت الأنقاض	Refugee	نازح
Strong waves	أمواج عاتية	Erosion	الانهيارات الأرضية
Exceeded	تجاوز		

1. Describe the magnitude of the Earthquake.

   ....

   ....

2. What are the refugees' needs?

   ....

   ....

   ....

28.2   *Provide a summary in Arabic for the above text.*

....

....

....

....

....

....

....

....

....

....

....

....

....

....

....

....

....

....

28.3 *Provide the equivalents of the underlined words/phrases in Arabic and use them in sentences.*

The <u>death toll</u> in Pakistan and the Pakistani controlled Kashmir province <u>has now reached</u> at least 20,000, in addition to hundreds killed in India and Afghanistan, due to an <u>earthquake that hit</u> the region on Saturday.

Tens of thousands of <u>those affected</u> by the earthquake in <u>the mountainous areas of northern Pakistan</u> have spent their second night without shelter.

The Pakistani interior minister, Aftab Sherpao, said in <u>a press conference</u> that more than 42,000 people were injured, and that the number is rising 'by the hour'.

The <u>survivors</u> in <u>several remote villages</u> are still <u>without shelter</u>, medicine, food supplies and clean water.

Amjad Anwar, an <u>elderly inhabitant</u> of the village of Patal, near Balakot, said: 'We don't want helicopters <u>hovering over us</u>. All we want is <u>blankets and water</u>.'

Pakistani officials said that the north-west frontier was the <u>worst affected</u> by the earthquake, as well as the Pakistani-<u>controlled</u> Kashmir province. The press reported that more than 400 children were killed when two schools <u>collapsed</u> in the north-west frontier. The Indian interior ministry said that many villages were <u>flattened in the earthquake,</u> and more than 600 people were killed in the Indian part of Kashmir.

The BBC's correspondent in Sirinjar, the summer capital of Indian-controlled Kashmir, <u>reported</u> that the local government is currently working on <u>reinstating</u> basic services, such as electricity and water.

Rescue efforts
In the capital Islamabad, people have begun <u>to dig through the</u> <u>debris</u> with their bare hands <u>to rescue survivors</u> trapped under the rubble of a building. British specialists joined Pakistani <u>rescue</u> workers, who <u>pulled a man</u> and a woman alive from <u>the rubble</u>.

....

....

....

....

....

....

....

....

....

....

....

....

....

....

....

....

....

....

....

....

....

28.4 *Translate the following Arabic text into English.*

الكوارث الطبيعية: تعريفها وأنواعها

تتغير المنظومات البيئية التي تعرفها سابقا بفعل الإنسان إما سلبيا أو إيجابيا لكن الطبيعة مهما قويت تطلعات الإنسان للتحكم فيها وتحويلها لصالحه، تظل باسطة سلطانها الذي يتخذ مظهرا غير متوقع وذي أضرار كبيرة، تلك هي الكوارث الطبيعية، فهي مجرد ظاهرة ككل الظواهر الطبيعية التي تنساب جوف وسطح كوكب الأرض.

معرفة مفهوم الكوارث الطبيعية ومخاطرها:

1- معرفة الكوارث ذات الأصل المناخي:

تتجلى هذه الكوارث ذات الأصل المناخي في الفيضانات المحلية والعواصف الثلجية، والحرائق الناتجة عن الجفاف ثم الأعاصير التي هي زوابع تدور فيها الرياح المحملة برطوبة كبيرة بسرعة تتراوح ما بين 120 و 300 km/h حول منطقة هادئة تسمى عين الإعصار وتتكون بالعروض المدارية التي تتجاوز بها حرارة السطح 72°

كما تنتج عن العواصف عواقب وخيمة مثل عاصفة 1999 بفرنسا التي خلفت ورائها 003 مليون شجرة مقتلعة- ضياع 70 % من المخزون الوطني من الأخشاب- مئات الأفراد تعرضوا للموت وخاصة في الغابات.

وكذا الإعصار يخلف عواقب خطيرة مثل إعصار Mitch 1998; الذي خلف 11677 ضحية

http://ejabat.google.com/ejabat/thread?tid=3b14148b1a440a73 (accessed 22 July 2013)

147

....

....

....

....

....

....

....

....

....

....

....

....

....

....

 28.5   *Summarise the following Arabic text into English.*

الأخطار الطبيعية

الأخطار الطبيعية هي الظواهر الجوية والمناخية القاسية والمتطرفة التي تحدث بصورة طبيعية في شتى أنحاء العالم، مع تعرض بعض المناطق، أكثر من غيرها، لأخطار معينة. وتُعد الأخطار الطبيعية كوارث طبيعية إذا ما تسببت في القضاء على حياة الإنسان وسبل العيش. والخسائر التي تتسبب فيها الكوارث الطبيعية، سواء كانت بشرية أو مادية، عقبة كأداء في طريق التنمية المستدامة. ويمكن حماية الأرواح والممتلكات من خلال إصدار تنبؤات وإنذارات دقيقة في شكل يسهل فهمه، وكذلك من خلال تعليم الجمهور كيفية التأهب للأخطار قبل أن تتحول إلى كوارث.

وتقوم المنظمة (WMO) بتوحيد وتنسيق أنشطة الحد من مخاطر الكوارث مع المنظمات الدولية والإقليمية والوطنية الأخرى، كما تقوم بتنسيق الجهود التي تبذلها المرافق الوطنية للأرصاد الجوية والهيدرولوجيا (NMHSs) من أجل الحد من الخسائر في الأرواح والممتلكات من خلال تحسين خدمات التنبؤ والإنذار المبكر وتقييم المخاطر، وكذلك من أجل إذكاء وعي الجمهور.

وينصب التركيز في عملية الحد من مخاطر الكوارث على أن: استثمار دولار واحد على التأهب للكوارث يمكن أن يحول دون وقوع خسائر اقتصادية متصلة بالكوارث قدرها سبعة دولارات – وهو عائد استثماري كبير. وتهدف المنظمة (WMO) إلى تخفيض متوسط عدد الوفيات التي حدثت بسبب الكوارث الطبيعية المتصلة بالطقس والمناخ والماء في السنوات العشر المنقضية بين عام 1994 وعام 2003 بنسبة 50 في المائة بحلول عام 2019. وتحدث الأخطار الطبيعية على نطاقات زمنية ومكانية مختلفة، وكل منها فريد في طبيعته. فتتسم أعاصير التورنيدو والفيضانات الخاطفة بأنها ظواهر قصيرة المدة ولكنها عنيفة تؤثر على مناطق صغيرة نسبياً. وبخلاف ذلك، فالجفاف مثلاً يستشري ببطء ولكنه يمكن أن يؤثر على معظم أنحاء قارة من القارات وعلى جميع السكان لشهور أو حتى لسنوات. ويمكن أن تنطوي ظاهرة جوية متطرفة على أخطار عديدة في آن واحد، أو تنطوي على أخطار متعددة سريعة التعاقب. ويمكن أن تؤدي العواصف المدارية، وكذلك الرياح الشديدة والأمطار الغزيرة إلى حدوث فيضانات وانهيالات وحلية. وفي خطوط العرض المعتدلة، يمكن أن يكون الطقس القاسي في فصل الصيف (العواصف

الرعدية والبرقية أو أعاصير التورنيدو) مصحوباً ببَرَد كثيف وفيضانات خاطفة. وقد تسهم أيضاً العواصف الشتوية المصحوبة برياح شديدة وثلوج غزيرة أو أمطار متجمدة في حدوث تيهورات في بعض المنحدرات الجبلية وفي حدوث جريان سطحي وفيضانات شديدة لاحقة في موسم الذوبان.

ويقع على عاتق بعض المرافق الوطنية للأرصاد الجوية والهيدرولوجيا والمراكز المتخصصة مسؤولية تقصي الأخطار الجيوفيزيائية، بما في ذلك الانفجارات البركانية (الرماد المنقول عن طريق الجو) والأمواج السنامية والمواد الخطرة المحمولة جواً (النويدات المشعة والمواد البيولوجية والكيميائية) والتلوث الحضري الحاد.

الجفاف

السبب الأساسي لأي حالة جفاف هي قلة هطول الأمطار. فالجفاف يختلف عن غيره من الأخطار، فهو يمتد ببطء وأحياناً على مدى سنوات، ويمكن أن تستتر بدايته وراء عدد من العوامل. وقد يكون للجفاف آثار مدمرة: منها نضوب مصادر المياه، وتوقف نمو المحاصيل، ونفوق الحيوانات، وسوء التغذية، واعتلال الصحة، التي تصبح أموراً واسعة الانتشار.

http://www.wmo.int/pages/themes/hazards/index_ar.html (accessed 22 July 2013)

....
....
....
....
....
....
....
....
....
....
....
....
....
....
....
....
....
....
....

....

....

....

....

....

....

....

....

....

....

....

....

....

....

....

....

....

....

MODULE REVIEW EXERCISES

1. Select the correct Arabic translation from the brackets for the underlined words.

There are international and <u>regional forces</u> (قوات إقليمية – قوات دولية – قوات أجنبية) that seek <u>to restore</u> (إعادة التشكيل – الحفاظ – استعادة) the policies and personalities of the <u>defunct regime</u> (النظام الفاشل – النظام الفاسد – النظام البائد). They realise that the Arab people will <u>regain their independence</u> (إعادة استقلالهم – إعادة قوتهم –) – and a greater political, cultural and economic unity – if the Arab spring is completed. To these forces we say: the differences of opinion between the political parties will only produce increased <u>co-operation</u> (زيادة التعاون – زيادة التضامن – زيادة التكامل) for the greater good of our country; and the <u>stability</u> (الاستقرار – التوازن - التفاؤل) of Egypt, <u>its transition</u> (تحولها – تغييرها – برمجتها) to democracy and building of a democratic society in <u>tandem with</u> (إلى جنب مع – بالإضافة إلى – مع ذلك) other Arab states, especially in North Africa, will have positive effects on the Mediterranean basin, Europe and the world.

http://www.theguardian.com/commentisfree/2011/nov/30/egypt-victor-election-democracy (accessed 25 November 2013)

2. Read the following Arabic translation and find out the words/phrases that have an opposite meaning to the English text below.

● ● ●

 http://www.guardian.co.uk/world/2011/feb/03/egypt-regime-death-toll-tahrir

'The Egyptian government is employing a strategy of eliminating witnesses to their actions,' said Mohamed Abdel Dayem, the regional coordinator of the Committee to Protect Journalists, reflecting fears that the crack-down presaged an all-out attack on the protesters.

The US administration also denounced what it described as 'systematic targeting' of the media. The US state department spokesman, PJ Crowley, said: 'There is a concerted campaign to intimidate journalists in Cairo and interfere with their reporting. We condemn such actions.'

Human rights workers were also detained when police raided a law centre in Cairo. Staff from Amnesty International and Human Rights Watch were among those picked up and their whereabouts were unknown.

The government combined the crack-down with political concessions aimed at drawing the sting from the revolt. The prime minister, Ahmed Shafiq, acknowledged that the attacks on anti-government protesters 'seemed to have been organised', and promised an investigation.

(accessed 20 August 2012)

151

Arabic translation

ومن جانبه قال محمد عبد الدايم المسئول الإقليمي للجنة حماية الصحفيين إن الحكومة المصرية تتبع إستراتيجية لاحتواء الشهود الذين يراقبون ما تفعله، وهو ما يقلل المخاوف من قيامها بتخفيظ هجماتها على المحتجين ضد الرئيس مبارك.

وقد أشادت الولايات المتحدة بما وصفته استهداف ممنهج لوسائل الإعلام، وفقا لتأكيدات المتحدث باسم الخارجية الأمريكية بي جي كراولي، والذي قال "هناك حملة منظمة لتشجيع الصحفيين في القاهرة، ودعمهم للقيام بعملهم، ونحن نشيد بمثل هذه التصرفات."

ولم يسلم العاملين بمنظمات حقوق الإنسان من الاستهداف، حيثتم تسريحهم من جانب الشرطة في وسط القاهرة، ومن بين المعتقلين عاملين بمنظمة العفو الدولية و هيومان رايتس ووتش، وتم اقتيادهم إلى أماكن معروفة.

ومن جانبه اعترف رئيس الوزراء المصري السابق أحمد شفيق بالأخطاء التي ارتكبت، وقال "الهجوم على المعتصمين أمر غير مقبول ويبدو انه كان مرتبا له"، ووعد شفيق بإجراء تحقيق رسمي فيما ما حدث.

---

3. *Remove any irrelevant translation and add additional information to the Arabic translation below, without distorting the original meaning of the following English text.*

---

http://www.guardian.co.uk/commentisfree/2012/feb/06/syria-massacres-hama

Last Friday, Syrian protesters rallied under the slogan 'forgive us Hama, we apologise'; a clear reference to the abject silence that has overshadowed that massacre throughout the last three decades. Although Hama was an ever-present bleeding wound in the Syrian popular conscience, and a humiliating disgrace that shook their souls, people were prohibited from remembering or mentioning it throughout the entire period of Hafiz al-Assad's rule. When his son assumed power in 2000, many were optimistic that he would at least give some consideration to the victims or reveal the fate of the thousands who were swallowed up in the prisons. But the young president chose to follow in his father's footsteps; he perpetrated another massacre in Hama and many others in Homs and other Syrian cities and towns. However, this time Bashar al-Assad has miscalculated. The Syrian revolution, which has so far sacrificed more than 7,000 dead, will not end unless the regime is overthrown.

(accessed 8 February 2012)

Arabic translation

أطلق المحتجون السوريون الغاضبون على الجمعة الماضية شعار (عذرا حماة سامحينا) في إشارة إلى الصمت المطبق الذي أحاط بتلك المجزرة والتي ذهب ضحيتها أشخاص من كل الأعمار خلال العقود الثلاثة الماضية، ومع أن حماة كانت حاضرة جرحا نازفا في الوجدان الشعبي السوري وشرخا غائرا في أعماق الذاكرة، وصمتا مهينا زلزل النفوس والضمائر، إلا أن الناس كانوا ممنوعين من تذكرها أو التفوه بشيء عنها طوال حكم الأسد الأب، ولما تسلم الابن السلطة استبشر البعض خيرا بأن بشار الأسد سيرد للضحايا بعض اعتبار أو يكشف للأبناء والزوجات عن مصير آلاف الذين ابتلعتهم سجون السلطة ولم يعرف شيء عنهم طوال تلك المدة، لكن الرئيس الشاب آثر أن يحمل أوزار أبيه، وأن يقتدي به، فصنع هو الآخر حماة ثانية وحمصا أخرى، مستفيدا من تعقيدات

المشهد الإقليمي والدولي، لكنه أخطأ الحساب هذه المرة، فثورة الشارع السوري الذي قدم حتى الآن أكثر من ستة آلاف قتيل لن تتوقف قبل إسقاط النظام .

---

4. Comment on the following Arabic translation taking into consideration the following:

- The selection of lexis: is the choice of words appropriate to the context?
- Is the translation of the culture-specific items appropriate?
- Is the grammar in the Arabic text correct?

Hafiz al-Assad's regime managed to get away with the massacre of Hama in 1982 because of the international silence dictated by the balance of forces during the cold war and a media blackout, which denied the victims a voice and prevented them from presenting the images of their calamity.

It is true that the regional and international balance of power continues to play a negative role in ending the suffering of the Syrian people. But the Syrians – as other Arab people in Tunisia, Egypt, Libya and Yemen – have now become the most important actors in the flow of events. This would enable them to overcome all external factors in their quest for freedom from tyranny and repression.

http://www.theguardian.com/commentisfree/2012/feb/06/syria-massacres-hama (accessed 25 November 2013)

Arabic translation

استطاع نظام الأسد الأب أن يرتكب مجزرة حماة الأولى عام ٢٨٩١ بسبب الصمت الدولي الذي أملته توازنات الحرب الباردة، وبسبب التعتيم الإعلامي الذي رافق تدمير المنازل والمساجد والمدارس، تعتيم حرم الضحايا من أن يكون لهم صوت أو أن تنقل مأساتهم . صحيح أن التوازنات الإقليمية والدولية لا تزال تلعب دورا سلبيا في إنهاء معاناة الشعب السوري، غير أن الشعب السوري اليوم، كما الشعوب العربية في تونس ومصر وليبيا واليمن، قد صار اللاعب الأهم في مسار الأحداث، وهو ما سيمكنه من تجاوز كل الحسابات والتوازنات الخارجية في سبيل الانعتاق من التسلط والقهر.

---

5. Paraphrase the following paragraph into Arabic in no more than 60 words.

It is equally important that political parties and independent candidates declare their acceptance of the election results. Any objections to election results should be made through constitutional mechanisms while maintaining calm in the constituencies and Egyptian street. This would send a clear message to those who wait to ambush Egypt, internally and externally: a message that we have begun a new phase in our political lives. We abide by the rules of democracy, and accept the will of the people. There will be winners and losers. But the real – and only – victor is Egypt.

http://www.theguardian.com/world/2011/nov/28/egypt-voters-record-numbers (accessed 10 April 2013)

....

....

....

....

....

....

 6. *Translate the following text into Arabic, using communicative translation (see Lesson 4).*

http://www.guardian.co.uk/world/2011/nov/28/egypt-voters-record-numbers?intcmp=239

Egypt election: voters defy fears of violence with record turnout

Fears of violence and chaos unfounded with no major violations or security incidents reported in first free ballot for over 80 years.

Egyptians came out to vote in record numbers, defying widespread predictions of violence and chaos and fears that the country was yet to break free from three stagnant decades of dictatorship.

Polls were kept open two hours past their scheduled closing time to allow long queues of people at polling stations throughout Cairo to cast their ballots. The high turnout followed 10 days of resurgent protests in the capital that had threatened to overshadow the election.

Egypt's military rulers and the high election commission, which is supervising the voting, reported no major violations or security incidents during the historic vote – the first free parliamentary ballot for more than 80 years.

However, some candidates are claiming irregularities outside several booths, which they allege will boost votes for the Muslim Brotherhood, the bloc likely to do best when the first round of votes in a three-stage process are counted.

The scene of the renewed uprising, Tahrir Square, was largely empty as long queues snaked outside schools and government offices around the city. Many of the demonstrators who had gathered in the square to demand the immediate departure of the supreme council of the armed forces (Scaf), the military junta that took power when President Hosni Mubarak was ousted in January, had urged a boycott of the election, claiming it was being set up to fail.

However, in those neighbourhoods where support for the largely liberal Tahrir movement was strongest, few people appeared to have listened. 'I came to vote because it is an opportunity that we can't miss,' said Hala Boutros.

(accessed 10 June 2013)

....

....

....

....

....

....

....

....

....

....

....

....

....

....

....

....

....

....

....

....

....

....

....

....

....

....

7. *Summarise the following paragraphs into Arabic.*

And move it did – slowly – throughout a well-mannered and patient day in an area that was widely predicted to stay at home, fearing that a still immature political system could not support a democratic transition in the nine troubled months since Mubarak was removed from power.

'For 30 years my parents' generation said they were denied a voice,' said Mona el-Eltawy, also in the women's queue in Zamalek. 'So I've come here on behalf of my family. If we don't vote we lose.'

Across the Nile in the impoverished Bulaq Abu Ela area, a muddy brown street outside a local schoolyard was being used for an impromptu town hall meeting by supporters from all blocs, who defied bans on handing out flyers to arriving voters. 'It means a lot to be here,' said one man, who appeared confused by the touts bidding for his vote. 'I can vote for who I want to, and I have faith that the process will be fair.'

http://www.theguardian.com/world/2011/nov/28/egypt-voters-record-numbers
(accessed 10 April 2013)

....

....

....

....

....

....

....

....

....

 8. *Translate the following underlined phrases and sentences into Arabic.*

The elections are finally being held following a referendum in March that approved a series of constitutional amendments and endorsed the junta-sponsored transition timetable that should have seen a parliamentary vote take place by September at the latest. As transition deadlines slipped, patience among many Egyptians ebbed and a fear grew that the Scaf was instead trying to hang on to power. The waning trust led to the reoccupation of Tahrir Square and fears that vote would not take place.

Preliminary results are expected later this week. Two further rounds of voting will be held in other areas of Egypt, the last on 3 January, before a 498-member lower house of parliament is elected. Its main task will be to form a committee to draft Egypt's new constitution, which promises to be a bitterly contested blueprint for the future.

http://www.theguardian.com/world/2011/nov/28/egypt-voters-record-numbers
(accessed 25 November 2013)

....

....

....

....

....

....

....

....

....

....

---

9.   Comment on the following Arabic translation of the English text below, taking into consideration the following:

- *The accuracy of the translation.*
- *The accuracy of the grammatical construction in the Arabic text below.*
- *Strategies used in the translation*

● ● ●

(◄ ►)   http://www.ikhwanweb.com/article.php?id=29278

The Egyptian elections have begun despite the many attempts to abort, obstruct or derail them. Millions of voters are electing a parliament to express their will and authority. We are about to accomplish the most important aims of the revolution: the building of a real democratic system, after getting rid of – or almost – the repressive dictatorship.

The military council has so far honoured its pledge to hold elections and protect them. It should continue the process to the end and accept the results, and the rights and powers of parliament. It is impossible for millions of Egyptians to go to the polls and vote for a parliament without authority. So the military council must now announce the handover of legislative powers to parliament, and the caretaker government must present any new legislation to the parliament for approval.

(accessed 25 November 2013)

....

....

....

....

....

....

Arabic translation

وبدأت الانتخابات في موعدها رغم كل المحاولات التي جرى لإجهاضه أو تعويقه أو إفساده.

صوت المصريين في الخارج في المرحلة الأولى، وكان أملاً تحقق رغم ضيق الوقت. وسط إقبال غير مسبوق يمكن يصل إلى 70% أي حوالي 53 مليون ناخب بمعدل يزيد على 12 مليون في كل مرحلة على الجميع أن يدرك حقيقة ساطعة ، وهى أن الشعب والملايين التي انتخبت لم تكن تعبث ولكنها تختار برلماناً يعبر بالبلاد من عنق الزجاجة ، يتحمل مسئولياتها الدستورية المعروف وفقاً للقواعد المستقرة للقواعد الديمقراطية ، ويعبر عن إرادة الشعب وسيادته التي هو جوهر النظم الدستورية .

نحن أمام استكمال أهم أهداف الثورة ، وهى البدء في بناء نظام ديمقراطي حقيقي بعد تخلصنا – أو كدنا –من نظام ديكتاتوري وإذا وصلت نسب التصويت إلى ما هو متوقع رغم كل المخاوف ، وبدأت النتائج في الظهور للمقاعد الفردية ومؤشرات للقوائم الحزبية وتحمل الشعب مسئولية الاختيار.

---

10. *Translate the following passage into Arabic, using the future tense.*

---

http://www.theguardian.com/world/2011/nov/28/egypt-voters-record-numbers

Across the Nile in the impoverished Bulaq Abu Ela area, a muddy brown street outside a local schoolyard was being used for an impromptu town hall meeting by supporters from all blocs, who defied bans on handing out flyers to arriving voters. 'It means a lot to be here,' said one man, who appeared confused by the touts bidding for his vote. 'I can vote for who I want to, and I have faith that the process will be fair.'

The high election commission said at a media conference it was not alarmed by the breach of the ban on campaigning, or distributing flyers within 48 hours of the poll. It had received numerous complaints about the breaches, which are thought to have been widespread and by all parties.

(accessed 25 November 2013)

....

....

....

....

....

....

....

....

....

....

Administrative Texts

Administrative texts are associated with the governing bodies of any entity, from large countries to small companies. They include documents associated with the legal issues of such bodies, for example the regulations of a company or the responsibilities of a job (job descriptions). Therefore, they are usually linked with legal texts. Legal and administrative language features are very similar, and will be discussed at length in the following module.

Most of the vocabulary used in these texts includes terms of speech and idioms which are usually associated with courts and public authorities. Undoubtedly, these texts are very formal, without much use of literary features. In addition, they differ from language to language, so the translator is advised to become acquainted with the terminology of the texts of both the SL and TL.

But for the most part, administrative texts have a relatively strict language style that can easily be translated, as it contains a lot of tabular information with shorter phrases which do not require complicated translation strategies, as will be shown in the various examples given here as drills. It is also close to legal language because it deals with formal sets of rules or regulations to be followed and administered in the entity concerned. This language is characterised by a formal tone and manner which uses a lot of modal auxiliaries (Thorne 1997). Paragraphs may be marked numerically with various possible sub-divisions. All these features will be highlighted in Module 7, regarding legal texts.

LESSON 29: TRANSLATING GUIDELINES AND REGULATIONS

Translating guidelines and regulations can be very technical as it may involve using specific terminologies and phrases. Such texts have a very limited style and specific meanings that should be carefully handled when translating into another language.

 29.1 *Summarise the following text into Arabic.*

GUIDELINES AND REGULATIONS

Students in all Middle Eastern Studies degree programmes except the BA (Hons) in A Modern Language and a Middle Eastern Language must write a dissertation as part of the final assessment for their degree.

A. GENERAL AIMS AND OBJECTIVES
The dissertation provides students with an opportunity to engage in a defined research project and to produce a substantial piece of work with a sustained focus. The aim of the dissertation is thus to foster independent study through:

- the identification of a particular theme or problem
- the identification of appropriate sources
- the development of a sustained and balanced argument based on those sources, leading to a conclusion.

In writing the dissertation students will apply, develop and extend the analytical and critical skills that they have acquired in earlier stages of the programme. As for essays, students will need to follow the appropriate scholarly conventions in terms of presentation, bibliography, footnotes and references. Detailed guidelines are available from the convenors of MEST 30000 or MEST 30010.

In fulfilling the requirements for a satisfactory dissertation, students will have demonstrated that they can identify a subject that is worthy of in-depth investigation and that they can independently master a substantial body of complex material, articulating their findings by means of a clear, consistent and analytical argument in a manner that is appropriate to the discipline. Students will also have demonstrated high levels of motivation and discipline, as the student input of 200 hours (10 hours per credit) for MEST 30010 (20 credit dissertation) or 400 hours (10 hours per credit) for MEST 30000 (40 credit dissertation in Modern Middle Eastern History) represents a substantial commitment of time and energy, equivalent to five (ten) 40-hour weeks devoted solely to the dissertation. (http://www.bio.txtshr.com/docs/index-4037.html?page=26)

 **Glossary**

Dissertation	أطروحة	Final assessment	التقييم النهائي

....
....
....
....
....
....
....
....
....
....
....
....
....
....
....
....
....
....

29.2   *Apply free translation strategy in your translation of the above text.*

....
....
....
....
....
....
....
....
....
....
....
....

....

....

....

29.3 Identify any inaccuracies in the Arabic translation below of the following English text.

Students in all Middle Eastern Studies degree programmes except the BA (Hons.) in A Modern Language and a Middle Eastern Language *must* write a dissertation as part of the final assessment for their degree. Students doing the BA (Hons.) in A Modern Language and a Middle Eastern Language *may* if they choose, write a dissertation as part of the final assessment for their degree.

A. General AIMS AND OBJECTIVES
The dissertation provides students with an opportunity to engage in a defined research project and to produce a substantial piece of work with a sustained focus. The aim of the dissertation is thus to foster independent study through:

- the identification of a particular theme or problem
- the identification of appropriate sources
- the development of a sustained and balanced argument based on those sources, leading to a conclusion.

Arabic translation

يتعين على الطلبة في جميع برامج شهادة الدراسات الشرق أوسطية كتابة أطروحة للتخرج كجزء من التقييم النهائي للحصول على شهادتهم، ويستثنى من ذلك طلبة درجة البكالوريوس (مرتبة الشرف) في برنامج بكالوريوس اللغة الحديثة ولغة الشرق الأوسط، ويحق لطلبة بكالوريوس (مرتبة الشرف) في اللغة الحديثة ولغة الشرق الأوسط كتابة هذه الأطروحة اختيارياً كجزء من التقييم النهائي لشهادتهم.

١. الأهداف العامة

تقدم الأطروحة للطلبة فرصة العمل على بحث محدد وإنتاج عمل هام ذو تركيز رصين، وتهدف الأطروحة بالتالي للتشجيع على الدراسة الذاتية من خلال:

- التعرف على فكرة أو مشكلة معينة
- التعرف على مصادر المعلومات المناسبة
- تقديم حجة قوية ومتزنة على أساس هذه المصادر وصياغة خاتمة لها

29.4 *Provide two main headings and two sub-headings in Arabic for the following text.*

You must do the following to ensure that the YouTube *Record from webcam* feature works:

- Log into your YouTube account
- Ensure that you have a working webcam built into or connected to your computer
- Select allow if asked to permit YouTube to access your camera and microphone

Once you have taken these preliminary steps, you can easily record and publish your webcam video.

1. If you don't see a picture in the record section, you may need to choose a different video source from the video dropdown in the *Record Video* window.
2. Once you see a picture coming from your camera, click the *Ready to Record* button to start recording your video.
3. When you're finished recording, click the red stop button.
4. You can preview your video before uploading by selecting the *Preview* button in the recording window.
5. If you are satisfied with your preview, click *Publish* to upload your video, or select *Re-record* to start over.

When you click the *Publish* button, your video will automatically be uploaded to YouTube and begin processing. You can edit information about the video by going to your my Videos page.

(http://carmenaboutsoftware.over-blog.com/categorie-12466962.html (accessed 25 November 2013)

1. ....

2. ....

3. ....

4. ....

29.5 *Identify and amend any inaccuracies in the Arabic translation below of the following English text.*

In fulfilling the requirements for a satisfactory dissertation, students will have demonstrated that they can identify a subject that is worthy of in-depth investigation and that they can independently master a substantial body of complex material, articulating their findings by means of a clear, consistent and analytical argument in a manner that is appropriate to the discipline. Students will also have demonstrated high levels of motivation and discipline, as the student input of 200 hours (10 hours per credit) for ARAB 3200 (20 credit dissertation) or 400 hours (10 hours per credit) for ARAB 32000

40) credit dissertation in Modern Middle Eastern History) represents a substantial commitment of time and energy, equivalent to five (ten) 40-hour weeks devoted solely to the dissertation.

Arabic translation

وحرصا على متطلبات الأطروحة الجيدة، فإنه يتعين على الطلبة عرض قدرتهم على تعريف موضوع مبني على العمل العميق وعلى تقديم ورقة بحثية ذات مواد مركبة، حيث تطرح ما توصلوا إليه من خلال تقديم حجة متكاملة وتحليلية بأسلوب يتلاءم مع فرع المعرفة. كما ينبغي على الطلبة إبداء مستويات عليا من البحث، حيث يتعين على الطالب إكمال 200 ساعة دراسية (10 ساعات لكل ساعة معتمدة) لمساق ARAB 3200 (20) ساعة معتمدة للأطروحة) أو 400 ساعة دراسية (10 ساعات لكل ساعة معتمدة) لمساق ARAB 32000 (40) ساعة دراسية معتمدة لأطروحة حول تاريخ الشرق الأوسط الحديث) بما يمثل التزاماً أساسيا من حيث الوقت، وهو ما يعادل 5 (10) 40 ساعة في الأسبوع لتقديم البحث فقط.

29.6 *Translate the following text into Arabic, using adaptation strategy.*

http://www.un.org/partnerships/Disclaimer.html

Using this site is subject to the following terms and conditions.

(a) The United Nations maintains this site (referred to as 'the site') for the benefit of those desiring information from it (referred to as 'users'). The nature of the available information on the site is considered purely informative. The United Nations has granted permission for users to visit the site and download information, documents and material (all of which are referred to as 'material') and copying it for personal and non-commercial use. Users do not have the right to resell the material, or redistribute it, or accumulate works derived from its source, or reproduce it. This is subject to terms and conditions set out below, and to more strict/specific restrictions applied to particular material on the site.

(b) This site is administered by the United Nations and is the source of all material contained therein.

The materials available in this site are 'as they are' introduced without warranty of any type, whether expressed or implied including without limits, warranties related to an appropriateness for display in commercial use, or specific to a particular purpose, or non infringement.

(accessed 15 March 2013)

Glossary

Purely informative	طبيعة إعلامية محضة	**Source of**	مصدرها
Granted permission	وتمنح الإذن	**Without any warranty**	دون تقديم أي نوع من أنواع الضمانات
Download information	تنزيل المعلومات	**Expressed or implied**	صريحة أو ضمنية
Non-commercial use	ليست للاستعمال التجاري	**Non-infringement**	عدم الانتحال
Accumulate works	تجميع أعمال		
Administered by	تدار من طرف		

....

....

....

....

....

....

....

....

....

....

....

....

....

....

LESSON 30: LEARNING AND TEACHING REGULATIONS

Translating this genre of texts is not a straightforward process, as it requires a substantial knowledge of the field of student education. Familiarity with such a register would help the translator to provide an accurate and reliable translation. Another challenge could be translating registers pertaining to Islamic education, as some of the terminologies may be very specific and associated with a particular school of thought or a religious sect. The translator would have to translate these culture-specific terminologies into the TL, without distorting the meaning of the ST. To overcome this challenge, awareness of the equivalence to these terminologies in the TL is vital in order to provide an acceptable translation. The style of such a register can be very limited in its use of rhetorical devices.

 30.1 *Provide a summary for the following text in Arabic.*

GENERAL TERMS OF ENGAGEMENT FOR GRADUATE TEACHING ASSISTANTS

1. All appointments are subject to the Charter, Statutes, Ordinances and Regulations of the University for the time being in force and to any conditions prescribed by the Council at the time of appointment.
2. Graduate Teaching Assistants are students of the University of XXX and are paid a maintenance grant by the University. They are also employed to teach a limited number of hours, the stipend for which is specified in the formal letter of appointment. The stipend is paid monthly, in arrears, through a bank account by direct credit transfer.
3. It is a condition of all appointments to Graduate Teaching Assistant posts that the person appointed must register for a higher degree by research at the University. The appointment will be terminated if the Graduate Teaching Assistant withdraws from or fails to re-register for the higher degree.
4. Graduate Teaching Assistants are responsible to their Deans of Faculty for the performance of their duties.
5. Graduate Teaching Assistants are required to undertake up to a maximum of 180 hours teaching in a year and, in addition, are required to undertake the necessary preparation, assessment and marking of such teaching. They are required to take part in any relevant training programmes as required by the University.
6. Other paid work may not be undertaken without the prior approval of the University Council. Persons who wish to take on other work should apply to their Deans of Faculty in the first instance.
7. Graduate Teaching Assistants may not enter into any negotiation, or make any representation, on behalf of the University in connection with any patent, invention, process or manufacture unless specifically authorised by the University to do so in any particular instance.

Glossary

Appointments	التعيينات	Necessary preparation	التحضيرات اللازمة
Statutes and ordinances	المراسيم واللوائح	Prior approval	موافقة مسبقة
Maintenance grant	منحة صيانة		

....

....

....

....

....

....

....

....

....

....

....

....

....

....

30.2 *Provide three main headings in Arabic for the above text.*

1. ....

2. ....

3. ....

30.3 *Provide the equivalent of the underlined words/phrases in Arabic, and use them in sentences.*

Graduate Teaching Assistants are students of the University and are paid a maintenance grant by the University. They are also employed to teach a limited number of hours, the stipend for which is specified in the formal letter of appointment. The stipend is paid monthly, in arrears, through a bank account by direct credit transfer.

It is a condition of all appointments to Graduate Teaching Assistant posts that the person appointed must register for a higher degree by research at the University. The appointment will be terminated if the Graduate Teaching Assistant withdraws from or fails to re-register for the higher degree.

....

....

....

....

....

....

....

....

....

....

....

30.4 *Provide synonyms in Arabic for the English underlined words and phrases, and identify three main features of the administrative text in the following paragraph.*

Graduate Teaching Assistants are required to inform the Faculty Human Resources Office, through their Deans of Faculty, of any periods of illness whether in semester or in vacation, during which they are eligible for Statutory Sick Pay or sickness benefit under the Housing Benefits and Social Security Acts. The amounts which they are entitled to receive as Statutory Sick Pay will be offset by the University against contractual sick pay (see separate statement) and recovered by the University from the Inland Revenue. Any sickness benefits payable by DSS after the expiry of Statutory Sick Pay will be deducted from salary. It is the responsibility of the individual Graduate Teaching Assistants to obtain the necessary Medical Certificates when required and to forward claims for sickness benefit to the Faculty Human Resources Office, not direct to DSS.

....

....

....

....

....

....

....

....

....

....

....

....

....

....

30.5 *Provide antonyms in Arabic for the following underlined words and phrases.*

فتح باب تقديم طلبات الالتحاق للفصل الثاني بالجامعة المفتوحة

أعلنت مساعد المدير للشئون الإدارية والمالية المكلف مسئول القبول والتسجيل في الجامعة العربية المفتوحة بالكويت الأستاذة منى اللوغاني أن فتح باب تقديم طلبات الالتحاق بالجامعة للفصل الدراسي الثاني للعام الجامعي 2010/2009 على فترتين. تبدأ الأولى يوم الأربعاء 2009/12/2 وحتى يوم الاثنين الموافق 2009/12/7 حيث يكون تعبئة طلب الالتحاق ودفع الرسوم الكترونيا عن طريق موقع الجامعة على شبكة الانترنت www.aou.edu.kw ولن يتم استقبال أي طلب ورقي خلال هذه الفترة.

وأضافت اللوغاني إن الفترة الدراسية الثانية فتتم خلال تسليم الوثائق المطلوبة إلى الموظف المختص في صالة القبول والتسجيل في مبنى الجامعة. ويتم تسليم إيصال يوضح فيه رقم طلب التقديم لافتة أن تاريخ 2009/12/8 سوف يخصص للحاصلين في شهادة الثانوية على نسبة من 80 % وما فوق أو ما يعادلها في نظام الأربع نقاط (من 3 إلى 4) نقاط بينما سيكون الأربعاء الموافق 2009/12/9 للحاصلين على شهادة الثانوية من نسبة 70% إلى أقل من 80% أو ما يعادلها في نظام الأربع نقاط (من 2.5 إلى أقل من 3) نقاط أما يوم الخميس الموافق 2009/12/10 سوف يخصص للحاصلين في الثانوية العامة على نسبة من 60 إلى أقل من 70% أو ما يعادلها في نظام الاربع نقاط من 2 إلى أقل من 5.2) نقطة حيث يتم ذلك خلال ساعات الدوام الرسمي من التاسعة صباحا وحتى الساعة الثانية ظهرا في كل من برنامج تقنية المعلومات والحوسبة وبرنامج الأدب الإنجليزي وآدابها وبرنامج إدارة الأعمال.

(http://www.alanba.com.kw/ar/kuwait-news/education/78779/26-11-2009)

....

....

....

....

....

....

....

....

1. Identify and correct the errors in the Arabic translation of the following English text.

Dear Candidate

Thank you for your interest in applying for this post. Your application should be in the following format:

- A completed Application Form (application forms should be completed fully and not replaced by a Curriculum Vitae, although you may wish to include your CV to support to your application)
- A completed Equal Opportunities Form
- A completed Disability Form

Applications are not usually acknowledged. If you wish your application to be acknowledged please return the enclosed postcard with stamp, affixed. Because of the large numbers of applications received by this office it is not possible to notify applicants if you have been unsuccessful. If you do not hear from the University within six weeks of the closing date please assume that you have been unsuccessful in your application.

Arabic translation

عزيزي المرشح

شكرا لاهتمامك في تطبيق لهذا المنصب. وينبغي أن يكون التطبيق الخاص بك على الشكل التالي :

- واستكمال تطبيق نموذج (ينبغي تعبئة استمارة تماما وليس الاستعاضة عن السيرة الذاتية ، على الرغم من أنك قد ترغب في أن تشمل السيرة الذاتية الخاصة بك لدعم التطبيق الخاص بك)
- استكمال وتكافؤ الفرص نموذج
- شكل العجز الانتهاء التطبيقات التي لا يعترف عادة. إذا كنت ترغب في التطبيق الخاص بك لا بد من الاعتراف الملصقة يرجى إعادة بطاقة بريدية المغلقة بخاتم. بسبب الأعداد الكبيرة من الطلبات التي تلقتها هذا المنصب ليس من الممكن أن تخطر المتقدمين إذا لم تكلل بالنجاح. إذا كنت لا تسمع من الجامعة في غضون ستة أسابيع من تاريخ إغلاق يرجى نفترض أن لديك لم تنجح في التطبيق الخاص بك.

2. Select the correct Arabic translation from the brackets for the underlined words in the following ST.

When arriving at an overall mark for a dissertation, <u>examiners</u> take into account a wide range of factors. Credit will be given for:

1. the identification of an <u>appropriate</u> theme, the nature of the overall approach to the subject and the relevance with which it is tackled

2. <u>clear</u> and coherent overall structure, with appropriate division into chapters which contribute to the progression of the argument as a whole

3. an introduction which contextualises the issues and sets down the <u>general line</u> of the approach which will follow

4. a clear and convincing line of argument, showing logic, consistency and intelligent handling of concepts, culminating in a conclusion

5. exploration and critical analysis of the issues and concepts <u>raised</u> in the dissertation topic

6. critical understanding of an appropriate breadth of research

7. appropriate use of examples, sources (primary and secondary), data, documentary evidence etc.

8. evidence of independent thought

9. good formal presentation (as per guidelines)

10. clear and appropriate discourse: correct use of language, including grammar, punctuation, spelling etc.

Arabic translation

ب. معايير التقييم

وفيما يتعلق بتحديد الدرجة الكلية للأطروحة، يأخذ (مراقبو ـ فاحصو ـ متتبعو) الأطروحة مجموعة واسعة من المعايير بعين الاعتبار، ويتم (التلخيص ـ التقييم – المراجعة) على النحو التالي:

1. تعريف الموضوع على (تماثل ـ نحو مناسب – مناسبة) ، وتعريف طبيعة المنهج الكلي المتبع في الموضوع وارتباطه بمشكلة البحث.

2. أن يتسم الهيكل العام للموضوع (بالوضوح – الصراحة – الإعتبار) والترابط المنطقي، وأن ينقسم إلى فصول مناسبة تساهم في تطور الحجة ككل.

3. عرض مقدمة تتضمن مشكلة البحث وتوضح (الخط العام – المنهج العام – السبيل العام) للمنهج المتبع.

4. صياغة الحجة على نحو واضح ومقنع، وأن تتسم بالمنطقية والانتظام وأن تثبت الإلمام بالمفاهيم على نحو جيد، وصولاً إلى الخاتمة.

5. استقراء وتحليل نقدي للقضايا والمفاهيم (المثارة – المناقشة – المطروحة) في موضوع الأطروحة.

6. فهم ناقد لعرض البحث على نحو مناسب.

7. الاستخدام المناسب للأمثلة والمصادر (الأولية والثانوية)، والبيانات و(الأمثلة ـ الأدلة – الأولية) الوثائقية، إلخ.

8. إثبات استقلالية الفكر.

9. تقديم عرض منهجي جيد (وفقاً للإرشادات)

10. صياغة واضحة ومناسبة للخطاب: استخدام صحيح للغة وقواعدها وعلامات الترقيم والإملاء، إلخ.

---

3. *Identify the major grammatical errors that have affected the Arabic translation below.*

Note: Presentation is a significant criterion in the assessment of a dissertation, and marks will be lost for failure to adhere to the guidelines, e.g. with respect to missing, incomplete or incorrect bibliographies; quotations without references or with incorrect or incomplete references; incorrect presentation of quotations; unacknowledged use of sources (plagiarism).

Arabic translation

ملاحظة: يعد التقديم معياراً هاماً لتقييم الأطروحة، وسيتم خصم الدرجات في حال عدم الالتزام الإرشادات مثل عدم تضمين فهرسه أو تقديمه ناقصا أو غير صحيحا، أو في حال إضافة اقتباس دون إشارة إلى المراجع أو تقديم مراجع غير صحيحة أو ناقصة، أو عرض اقتباسات على نحو خاطئ، أو في حال استخدام مصادر دون تعريفها (السرقة الأدبية).

---

4. Replace the underlined words with Arabic synonyms in the following translation, without distorting the meaning of the ST.

وفيما يتعلق بتحديد الدرجة <u>الكلية</u> للأطروحة، يأخذ فاحصو الأطروحة مجموعة <u>واسعة</u> من المعايير بعين الاعتبار، ويتم <u>التقييم</u> على النحو التالي:

- تعريف الموضوع على <u>نحو</u> مناسب، وتعريف <u>طبيعة</u> المنهج <u>الكلي</u> المتبع في الموضوع <u>وارتباطه بمشكلة البحث</u>.
- أن <u>يتسم</u> الهيكل العام للموضوع بالوضوح <u>والترابط</u> المنطقي، وأن ينقسم إلى فصول مناسبة <u>تساهم</u> في تطور <u>الحجة</u> ككل.
- عرض مقدمة تتضمن مشكلة البحث <u>وتوضح</u> الخط العام للمنهج المتبع.
- <u>صياغة الحجة</u> على نحو واضح و<u>مقنع</u>، وأن تتسم بالمنطقية <u>والانتظام</u> وأن تثبت <u>الإلمام</u> بالمفاهيم على نحو جيد، وصولاً إلى الخاتمة.
- <u>استقراء</u> وتحليل نقدي للقضايا والمفاهيم <u>المثارة</u> في موضوع الأطروحة.

---

5. The translation below inaccurately reflects the meaning of the following English text. Rewrite the text, correcting the inaccuracies in the translation.

Section D: General Statement

Please attach a general statement relating to the introduction of the programme of study which should address the following issues as appropriate:

- the place of the proposal within the University's and department's overall teaching portfolio and whether it represents consolidation, strengthening or new directions
- the national context of the proposal including, for example, evidence of student demand, national need, distinctiveness, academic importance, existing provision at other universities other features prompting the proposal
- the department's overall view of the proposal
- the relationship of the programme content to its stated learning outcomes
- the range of teaching methods to be used, drawing attention to any innovative practices
- assessment procedures, their relationship to faculty norms and any innovative practice
- the degree of conformity to faculty norms in respect of elective elements, structure of joint honours programmes etc.
- arrangements for supervision of projects, fieldwork
- departmental programme management structure and arrangements for review.

When appropriate, for programmes including a year abroad:

- information on language training should be supplied. This should be an integral part of the programme. Information on how language competence will be assessed and a plan of action identified for where competence is insufficient.

- information on what courses can be followed abroad should be supplied, and indications, using ECTS credits, etc., of how the work is commensurate with the credit rating assigned to the period abroad should be given. It should be demonstrated how work done abroad links with that done at Leeds in terms of providing pre-requisites for further study or avoiding duplication.
- information on assessment and use in classification of work abroad should be supplied and where appropriate an indication of what work has been done to establish equivalence of marking scales should be given.

http://www.leeds.ac.uk/aqst/approval/programme-spec-guidance.pdf (accessed 2 November 2010)

Arabic translation

فقرة د: البيان العام

برجاء وضع البيان العام المتعلق بتقديم المقرر الدراسي و الذي يجب أن يهتم بالمواد الآتية كما هو ملائم:
- وضع العرض في ملف التربية الشامل للجامعة و القسم و هل يمثل اتجاه جديد.
- المضمون الوطني للمقترح متضمنا، على سبيل المثال، الأدلة على الطلب من قبل طلاب، الاحتياج القومي، التميز، الأهمية الأكاديمية، تقديم نفس البرنامج في جامعات أخرى، ملامح أخرى في صالح البرنامج المقترح.
- النظرة المثالية للقسم على البرنامج المقترح.
- علاقة محتوى البرنامج بمخرجات التعلم المعترف بها.
- أنواع أساليب التدريس المقترحة، بتوجيه النظر نحو المعاملات الحديثة
- أساليب التقويم و علاقته بمقاييس الجامعة و أية ممارسات حديثة.
- درجة التماثل مع مقاييس الكلية فيما يتعلق بالعناصر الإجبارية و شكل البرامج الدراسية المشتركة إلخ
- ترتيبات مراقبة المشروعات و العمل الميداني
- هيكل إدارة القسم للبرنامج و تصميمات المواد

للبرامج التي تتضمن عام خارج البلد، كما هو ملائم:
- توفر المعلومات الخاصة بالتدريب على اللغة. يجب أن يكون هذا جزء لا يتجزأ من البرنامج. معلومات عن كيفية تقويم المستوى اللغوي و خطة عمل لمناطق الضعف في الجدارات.
- يجب توافر معلومات عن الدورات التي يمكن إتباعها خارج الدولة و الدلائل، مستخدمين الساعات المعتمدة ECTS إلخ لكيفية معادلة الشغل المبرمج خلال العام الخارجي. يجب استعراض كيفية ربط العمل الخارجي بالعمل الذي تم إنجازه في ليدز فيما يتعلق بتوفير متطلبات مقدمة للدراسة الممتدة أو الابتعاد عن التكرار.
- توفر معلومات عن تصنيف العمل الخارجي و مؤشر للعمل الذي تم إنجازه لتأسيس معادلة لوضع الدرجات، عندما يكون ذلك ملائما.
- توفر معلومات عن الترتيبات الإدارية للتبادل. يجب إعطاء إقرارات لتوافر الدعم الكافي للطلاب في جامعة التبادل.

6. *Translate the following text and then comment on the strategies you followed.*

http://www.findlaw.co.uk/law/immigration_emigration/immigration_basics/30639.html

This page describes the different types of 'entry clearance', including visas, and explains who needs to apply for entry clearance before travelling to the UK.

There are 4 types of entry clearance that can give someone permission to travel to or enter the UK:

- A **visa** is for nationals of the countries or territories listed in Appendix 1 of the Immigration Rules (known as '**visa nationals**') – see 'More information' below.
- An **entry certificate** is issued to nationals of other countries outside the European Economic Area (EEA) and Switzerland (known as '**non-visa nationals**').
- An **EEA family permit** is issued to the family members of EEA nationals.
- An **exempt vignette** is issued to people who are exempt from the requirements of the Immigration Act 1971, such as diplomats.

On this website, **we use the term 'visa' to cover visas and entry certificates**.

The entry clearance process for the UK is operated by the UK Border Agency, through our overseas network.

The Channel Islands and the Isle of Man are not part of the UK and have their own immigration laws and policies, but our visa offices also issue visas for these islands.

Entry clearance requirements
You might need to obtain entry clearance **before** you travel to the UK, depending on your nationality and your reason for wanting to travel here.

You can use the 'Do you need a visa?' tool to find out whether you need a visa to come here.

If you are a visa national, you will need to obtain a visa before you come to the UK.

If you are a non-visa national, you might need to obtain a visa if you want to come to the UK for up to 6 months. You will need a visa if you want to come here for more than 6 months. For more information, see the Non-visa nationals page.

Some visa nationals do not need a visa if they want to 'transit' the UK for a short time on their way to another country – see the In transit through the UK pages.

You will not need a visa if you hold a passport issued by the UK or any other country in the European Economic Area (EEA), or Switzerland.

(accessed 20 August 2012)

....

....

....

....

....

....

....

....

....

....

....

....

....

....

....

....

....

....

....

....

....

....

....

....

....

....

7. Put the translated ideas of the following English text into a coherent and cohesive Arabic text, paying attention to the use of cohesive devices. Then correct any inaccuracies in the translation.

Generic skills

Threshold level
On graduating with an honours degree in area studies, students should have the ability to:

- identify and represent a range of issues and differing opinions
- identify and offer resolutions to relevant problems

- synthesise information and develop argument
- communicate ideas with clarity and coherence
- work independently and to deadlines within a guided framework
- respond to constructive feedback
- employ effective essay and report writing skills, showing ability to deploy material from a variety of sources
- develop collaborative skills in group work to achieve shared goals
- utilise proficiently a range of information technology resources, including word-processing, use email, search databases and text files, and locate and employ internet sites. (The Quality Assurance Agency for Higher Education 2008)

Arabic translation

المهارات العامة:

المستوي الأساسي

يجب أن يكون لدى الخريج، عند التخرج بمرتبة شرف في دراسات المنطقة، القدرة علي الآتي:

- تمييز وعرض نطاق من الموضوعات و الآراء المختلفة.
- تمييز وعرض حلول للمشاكل المتعلقة.
- توصيل الآراء بوضوح و تماسك.
- العمل باستقلالية ضمن إطار المواعيد النهائية وذلك من خلال هيكل عمل موجّه.
- الاستجابة للتغذية العكسية البناءة.
- توظيف مهارات الكتابة و التقرير بكفاءة و إظهار القدرة على استخدام مواد من مصادر متنوعة.
- تطوير مهارات تعاونية في العمل الجماعي من أجل تحقيق هدف مشترك.
- استخدام نطاق من مصادر تكنولوجيا المعلومات بكفاءة متضمنة معالجة الكلمات واستخدام البريد الإلكتروني و قواعد البيانات و ملفات البحث واستخدام مواقع الإنترنت.

....

....

---

8. Omit any redundant information in the Arabic translation of the following paragraph, and then comment on the strategies used in the translation.

Typical level

On graduating with an honours degree in area studies, students should have the ability to:

- critically analyse and demonstrate detailed knowledge of the area; its history, culture and society as defined by the programme provider
- demonstrate awareness and critical understanding of relevant vocabulary of contributory disciplines and critical theories, and the capacity to assess and compare the merits of contrasting approaches
- describe, differentiate and compare concepts from different disciplines and/or interdisciplinary approaches as a means of understanding the area under study
- demonstrate awareness of, and ability to use, evaluate and compare a diverse range of relevant information and research resources
- where relevant, acquire knowledge of a language as required by the degree programme concerned and apply these linguistic skills effectively at an appropriate level. (The Quality Assurance Agency for Higher Education 2008)

Arabic translation

المستوى النموذجي

يجب أن يكون لدى الخريج الجامعي في دراسات المنطقة، القدرة على الآتي:

- التحليل النقدي واظهار معرفة مفصلة عن المنطقة؛ تاريخها و ثقافتها و مجتمعها كما هو معرف من قبل مقدم البرنامج.
- اظهار وعي و فهم نقدي للمفردات الملائمة الخاصة بالمجالات المساهمة و النظريات النقدية و القدرة علي تقييم و مقارنة استحقاقات المناهج المتغايرة.
- وصف و تمييز و مقارنة المفاهيم الخاصة بالفروع الدراسية المختلفة و/أو منظور ما بين الفروع كوسيلة لفهم المنطقة تحت الدراسة.
- اظهار وعي وقدرة على استخدام و تقييم و مقارنة نطاق مختلف من المعلومات الملائمة و مصادر البحث.
- اكتساب معرفة باللغة كما هو مطلوب بموجب البرنامج الدراسي و تطبيق هذه المهارات اللغوية بكفاءة عند مستوى ملائم.

> 9. *Add additional information to the translation of the following English text, without distorting the meaning of the ST.*

Benchmark standards

Benchmark standards for area studies graduates are defined at 'threshold' and 'typical' levels of achievement. The threshold standard is the minimally acceptable attainment of an honours graduate. The standard expected of the majority of honours graduates is defined as the typical standard. Graduates at both levels will show knowledge and understanding of their area. Those at threshold level will do so by basic presentation of information, evidence and argument. Graduates at typical level will show abilities to evaluate information independently, to assess evidence critically, and to develop argument individually.

Subject-specific skills

Threshold level

On graduating with an honours degree in area studies, students should have the ability to:

- demonstrate knowledge of the area; its history, culture and society, as defined by the programme provider
- demonstrate awareness of relevant vocabulary and of contributory disciplines and theories
- describe concepts from different disciplines and/or interdisciplinary approaches as a means of understanding the area under study
- demonstrate awareness of a diverse range of relevant information and research resources
- where relevant, acquire knowledge of a language as required by the degree programme concerned. (The Quality Assurance Agency for Higher Education 2008)

Arabic translation

مقاييس المقارنة

يتم تعريف مقاييس المقارنة لخريجي المادة الدراسية عند مستويات إنجاز "أساسية" و "نموذجية". المقياس الأساسي هو أدنى مستويات الإنجاز المقبولة لخريج الجامعة. يتم تعريف المستوى المتوقع من معظم الخريجين بالمستوى "النموذجي". سوف يظهر خريجي كل من المستويين معرفة و فهم لمجال دراستهم. هؤلاء الذين عندهم المستوى "الأساسي" سوف يظهرون ذلك من خلال العرض الأساسي للمعلومات و الأدلة و النقاش. سوف يظهر خريجي المستوى "النموذجي" قدرات على تقييم المعلومات باستقلالية و تقييم الأدلة بأسلوب نقدي و تطوير نقاش بمفردهم.

مهارات خاصة بالمادة الدراسية

المستوى الأساسي

يجب أن يكون لدى الخريج الجامعي في دراسات ما، القدرة على الآتي:

- اظهار معرفة بالمنطقة؛ تاريخها و ثقافتها و مجتمعها كما تم تعريفه من قبل مقدم البرنامج
- اظهار الوعي بالمفردات الملائمة و المجالات و النظريات المساهمة.
- وصف المفاهيم الخاصة بالمجالات المختلفة و/أو النهج ما بين المجالات كوسيلة لفهم المنطقة التي تحت الدراسة.

استعراض الوعي بالنطاق المتنوع من المعلومات الملائمة و مصادر البحث.

اكتساب معرفة باللغة كما هو مطلوب بموجب الدرجة العلمية للبرنامج الدراسي، حين يكون ذلك ملائما.

---

10. *Comment on the Arabic translation of the following English text, taking into consideration:*

- *The selection of lexis. Is the choice of words appropriate to the context?*
- *The grammatical construction of sentences. Does it take into consideration the distinctive features of Arabic grammar?*
- *The strategies employed in the translation (see Module 1).*

Section C: External Review

The University of Leeds

External Review of a new programme of study

Department / School ....

Proposed Programme of Study ....

External Reviewer ....

Thank you for agreeing to act as external reviewer for this new programme of study. All programmes of study are subject to approval of the Learning and Teaching Committee of the relevant faculty. The committees work on the premise that the expertise on a subject rests in the proposing academic department and that any judgements it makes on the academic content of a proposed new programme must be limited. For this reason proposers are asked to seek a review from a peer in their subject area. We would welcome your comments in this spirit. You may wish to consider addressing the following:

Overall curriculum design

Subject content and skills covered

Assessment arrangements

Relationship of the proposals to other subject provision in the same area in the UK and the relevant QAA Subject Benchmark Statement(s)

Likely marketability and recruitment prospects

Likely employment of graduates

Signature .... **Date** ....

Please continue on additional sheet(s) if necessary. http://www.leeds.ac.uk/qat/policy procedures/index-of-forms.html

Arabic translation

الفقرة ج: المراجعة الخارجية

جامعة ليدز

مراجعة خارجية لبرنامج دراسي جديد

القسم/ الكلية: ....

البرنامج الدراسي المقترح: ....

المراجع الخارجي: ....

شكرا لموافقتك على أن تقوم بدور المراجع الخارجي لهذا البرنامج الدراسي الجديد. جميع البرامج الدراسية تخضع لموافقة لجنة التعلم والتدريس للكلية المعنية. تقوم اللجان بالعمل في مكان تواجد الخبرة الخاصة بالمادة في القسم الأكاديمي المقترح و أنه يحب أن تكون الأحكام الصادرة من قبل هذه اللجان على المحتوى الأكاديمي لبرنامج جديد مقترح محدودة. لذا فهو مطلوب من المقترحين السعي للحصول على مراجعة من نظير لهم في المجال الخاص بالمادة. سوف نرحب بملاحظاتك في ضوء هذه الروح. قد ترغب في مخاطبة الآتي:

- التصميم الشامل للمنهج
- محتوى المادة و المهارات المتضمنة
- ترتيبات التقييم
- علاقة البرنامج المقترح بالمواد الأخرى في نفس المنطقة ببريطانيا و المقاييس الملائمة لهيئة ضمان الجودة
- رجاحة التسويق و إمكانيات الالتحاق
- رجاحة حصول الخريجين على وظائف

التوقيع.......................... التاريخ ....

برجاء الاستكمال علي صفحات إضافية إذا لزم الأمر

Legal Texts

Legal language is known to be very strict and precise, with no freedom for a creative style. But although legal translation belongs to specialised translation, it shares some of the characteristics of general translation. It can be classified according to the functions of legal discourse and in connection to the legal discourse sub-types. Similar to other specialised translation texts, according to Reiss, legal texts serve 'an informative function' (cf. Šarčević, 1997: 7). Legal texts can have both directive and imperative function, as well as an expressive function (Newmark 1982). To Sager (1993), legal texts are informative for the general reader and directive for a specific group of people (El-Farahaty 2011: 35).

Types of legal texts

There are three different types of legal writing to be distinguished: (a) academic texts which consist of academic research journals and legal textbooks, (b) juridical texts covering court judgements or law reports and (c) legislative or statutory writings consisting of Acts of Parliament, contracts, treaties, etc. (Hiltunen 1990: 81). Legal texts are classified as follows:

- Legislative texts (e.g. domestic statutes, subordinate laws, international treaties and multilingual laws and other laws produced by law making authorities).
- Judicial texts produced in the judicial process by judicial officers and other legal authorities.
- Legal scholarly texts produced by academic lawyers or legal scholars in scholarly works and commentaries whose legal status depends on the legal systems in different jurisdictions.
- Private legal texts that include texts written by lawyers (i.e. contracts, leases, wills, etc.) (Cao 2007: 9–10, in El-Farahaty 2011: 33).

Legal texts may also be categorised into descriptive and prescriptive texts, in addition to hybrid texts which contain both functions (e.g. judicial decisions, appeals, petitions) (cf. Šarčević 1997: 11). The first type describes the course of the action that individuals ought to take and respect. This includes, for instance, laws, regulations, codes, contracts, treaties and conventions. The second group of legal texts involves judicial decisions, and instruments such as actions, pleadings, briefs, appeals, requests, petitions, etc. The third group of legal texts includes legal opinions, law textbooks, and articles (ibid.).

LESSON 31: TRANSLATING LEGAL TEXTS

These varied types of legal writing clearly reflect the complexity and diversity of the features that constitute legal texts, and such complexity makes their translation a challenging task. Therefore, even though we might believe that legal terms are rendered word-for-word, thereby making legal translation easy, the translation process is not in fact easy, especially because it is bound by culture and language. It is 'a translation from one legal system into another – from the source legal system into the target legal system' (Šarčević 1997:13), and it is this transfer which makes the process very complex.

It can be argued here that the translation of legal terminologies is the backbone of the legal translation. Translating these terminologies often requires a sound translation strategy, especially in contexts where some of these terminologies do not have equivalents in the TT. Terms should be translated as exactly as possible lest a change in the meaning causes undesirable legal consequences. This is especially true because these terms tend to be restricted in meaning and can only be used denotatively. Particular care should be taken with regard to synonyms or polysemous words. For example, the Arabic word *ḥukm* should be carefully studied before translating it to a possible English equivalent (decision, sentence, ruling, holding, verdict, etc.). Furthermore, certain words (such as *herewith*, *therefore*, *the consequences*), which are not strict terms, need also be translated literally using the known equivalents in the TL. Legal vocabulary is a 'primarily symbolic lexicon which places great stress upon the legal signifier or legal word as an entity in itself. It is a vocabulary of possibilities purportedly comprising a comprehensive system of meanings that are internal or latent within the lexicon itself (Goodrich 1987: 177). It is this complexity of legal vocabulary, as referred to above, that makes legal translation a challenging task. Alcaraz and Hughes (2002: 16–18) classify legal vocabulary into three sub-types:

1. Purely Technical Terms, which serve specific purposes, giving therein pure legal meaning.
2. Semi-Technical or Mixed Terms, which serve general purposes.
3. Everyday Vocabulary, which exists in legal texts without losing its everyday function and purpose (Alcaraz and Hughes 2002: 16–18).

In addition to requiring a sound knowledge of the specific nature of the language, the syntactic structures of legal texts can pose problems for translators, especially the level of nominal structures where peculiar legal syntax can be found. The prevalence of nominal constituents alongside long sentences, which contain subordinated clauses (Hiltunen 1990: 69), makes it particularly difficult to render into the TL. As we will see from the range of drills provided below, the syntactic structure of legal texts remains a challenge to translators.

31.1 *Summarise the following text in Arabic.*

---

http://www.gnu.org/licenses/dsl.html

TERMS AND CONDITIONS FOR COPYING, DISTRIBUTION AND MODIFICATION

Copyright © 1999–2001 Michael Stutz <stutz@dsl.org> Verbatim copying of this document is permitted, in any medium.

1. DEFINITIONS.
'License' shall mean this Design Science License. The License applies to any work which contains a notice placed by the work's copyright holder stating that it is published under the terms of this Design Science License.

'Work' shall mean such an aforementioned work. The License also applies to the output of the Work, only if said output constitutes a 'derivative work' of the licensed Work as defined by copyright law.

'Object Form' shall mean an executable or performable form of the Work, being an embodiment of the Work in some tangible medium.

'Source Data' shall mean the origin of the Object Form, being the entire, machine-readable, preferred form of the Work for copying and for human modification (usually the language, encoding or format in which composed or recorded by the Author); plus any accompanying files, scripts or other data necessary for installation, configuration or compilation of the Work.

'Author' shall mean the copyright holder(s) of the Work. The individual licensees are referred to as 'you.'

2. RIGHTS AND COPYRIGHT.
The Work is copyrighted by the Author. All rights to the Work are reserved by the Author, except as specifically described below. This License describes the terms and conditions under which the Author permits you to copy, distribute and modify copies of the Work.

In addition, you may refer to the Work, talk about it, and (as dictated by 'fair use') quote from it, just as you would any copyrighted material under copyright law.

Your right to operate, perform, read or otherwise interpret and/or execute the Work is unrestricted; however, you do so at your own risk, because the Work comes WITHOUT ANY WARRANTY.

(accessed 27 March 2012)

Glossary

License	الترخيص	Copying and modification	النسخ و التعديل
Under the terms	وفقا لأحكام	Accompanying	المرفقة
Aforementioned	الآنفة الذكر	Copyright	حقوق الطبع والنشر
As defined by law	وفقا للقانون	Copyright reserved	حقوق النشر محفوظة
Executable	قابل للتنفيذ	Unrestricted	غير مقيد

....
....
....
....
....
....
....
....
....
....
....
....
....
....
....
....
....
....
....

> *31.2   Identify and amend any inaccuracies in the Arabic translation of the following English text. Then comment on the strategies utilised in the translation of the following text.*

http://www.un.org/docs/sc/unsc_background.html

The Security Council has primary responsibility, under the Charter, for the maintenance of international peace and security. It is so organized as to be able to function continuously, and a representative of each of its members must be present at all times at United Nations Headquarters. On 31 January 1992, the first ever Summit Meeting of the Council was convened at Headquarters, attended by Heads of State and Government of 13 of its 15 members and by the Ministers for Foreign Affairs of the remaining two. The Council may meet elsewhere than at Headquarters; in 1972, it held a session in Addis Ababa, Ethiopia, and the following year in Panama City, Panama.

When a complaint concerning a threat to peace is brought before it, the Council's first action is usually to recommend to the parties to try to reach agreement by peaceful means. In some cases, the Council itself undertakes investigation and mediation. It may appoint special representatives or request the Secretary-General to do so or to use his good offices. It may set forth principles for a peaceful settlement.

(accessed 10 February 2013)

Arabic translation

يتولى مجلس الأمن، بشروط الميثاق، المسؤولية الأساسية عن الموافقة على السلام والأمن الدوليين. وهو منظم بحيث يستطيع العمل بدون توقف، ويجب أن يكون ممثل من كل واحد من أعضائه موجودا في مكان الأمم المتحدة طول الوقت. وفي 31 كانون الثاني/يناير 1992، عُقد أول اجتماع قمة للمجلس في المقر، وحضره رؤساء دول وحكومات 13 من أعضائه الـ 15 ووزيرا خارجية العضوين الآخرين. ويمكن للمجلس أن يجتمع في مكان غير المقر؛ ففي عام 1972، عقد دورة في أديس أبابا، إثيوبيا، وعقد في العام التالي دورة في مدينة بنما، بنما.

وعندما تصل إلى المجلس قضية تتعلق بخطر يتهدد السلام، يبدأ عادة بتقديم توصيات إلى الأطراف بمحاولة التوصل إلى اتفاق بالوسائل السلمية. وفي بعض الحالات، يضطلع المجلس نفسه بالعمل والوساطة. ويجوز له أن يعيّن ممثلين أجنبيين أو يطلب إلى الأمين العام أن يفعل ذلك أو يبذل إمكانياته الحميدة. كما يجوز له أن يضع مبادئ من أجل تسوية سلمية.

....

....

....

....

....

.... –

.... –

.... –

.... –

.... –

31.3 *Identify the translation errors in the Arabic translation of the following English texts.*

The Purposes of the United Nations are:

1. To maintain international peace and security, and to that end: to take effective collective measures for the prevention and removal of threats to the peace, and for the suppression of acts of aggression or other breaches of the peace, and to bring about by peaceful means, and in conformity with the principles of justice and international law, adjustment or settlement of international disputes or situations which might lead to a breach of the peace;

2. To develop friendly relations among nations based on respect for the principle of equal rights and self-determination of peoples, and to take other appropriate measures to strengthen universal peace;

3. To achieve international co-operation in solving international problems of an economic, social, cultural, or humanitarian character, and in promoting and encouraging respect for human rights and for fundamental freedoms for all without distinction as to race, sex, language, or religion; and

4. To be a centre for harmonizing the actions of nations in the attainment of these common ends.

http://www.un.org/en/documents/charter/chapter1.shtml (accessed 10 March 2013)

Arabic translation

مقاصد الأمم المتحدة هي:

1- حفظ السلم والأمن الدولي، وتحقيقاً لهذا الهدف تتخذ الهيئة القوانين المشتركة الفعّالة لمنع الأسباب التي تهدد السلم وانعدامها، وتقمع أعمال العدوان وغيرها من وجوه الإخلال بالسلم، وتتذرّع بالوسائل السلمية، حسبا لقوانين العدل والقانون الدولي، لحل الاختلافات الدولية التي قد تؤدي إلى الإخلال بالسلم أو لتسويتها.

2- إنماء العلاقات التفاهمية بين الأمم على أساس احترام المبدأ الذي يقضي بالتسوية في الحقوق بين الشعوب وبأن يكون لكل منها تحديد مصيرها، وكذلك اتخاذ التدابير الأخرى المناسبة لتقوية السلم العام.

3- خلق التفاعل الدولي على حل المسائل الدولية ذات الصبغة الاقتصادية والاجتماعية والثقافية والإنسانية وعلى تعزيز احترام حقوق الإنسان والحريات الثانوية للناس جميعاً والتشجيع على ذلك إطلاقاً بلا تمييز بسبب الجنس أو اللغة أو الدين ولا تفريق بين الرجال والنساء.

4- جعل هذه الهيئة مرجعاً لجمع أعمال الأمم وتقنينها نحو إدراك هذه المسائل المشتركة.

The UN does not make any specific warranties or statements with regards the accuracy of these materials or its completion. The UN regularly changes, improves, and updates the material shown without prior notification. The UN is not responsible under any circumstance for any loss, damage, liability, or expense as a result or claimed result of the use of this site, including without limit any error, mistake, omission, interruption, or delay in this respect. The User is fully responsible for the use of this site. The UN and her/its affiliated bodies/affiliates are not responsible under any circumstance from any direct, indirect, incidental or dependant loss, even when the UN has knowledge of the possibility of such a loss.

Arabic translation

ولا تقدم الأمم المتحدة أي بيانات تفيد تأييدها أو تبنيها لدقة أو موثوقية أي نصيحة أو رأي أو بيان أو غير ذلك من المعلومات المتاحة من قبل أي مقدم للمعلومات، أو مستعمل لهذا الموقع أو أي شخص أو كيان آخر. كما يكون المستعمل مسئولاً كامل المسؤولية عن اعتماده على مثل هذه النصائح أو الآراء أو البيانات أو غيرها من المعلومات. ولا تكون الأمم المتحدة أو هيئاتها الفرعية، أو أي من الوكلاء، أو الموظفين، أو مقدمي المعلومات أو كتاب محتوى الإنترنت التابعين لهما، مسئولة أمام أي مستعمل أو أي جهة أخرى عن أي خطأ، أو غلط أو إغفال أو انقطاع أو حذف أو عيب أو تغيير، في المحتوى أو عن استخدامه، أو تقديمه في الوقت المناسب أو اكتماله، وليستا مسئولتين عن أي قصور في الأداء أو أي فيروس حاسوبي أو انقطاع في خط الاتصال، مهما كان السبب في ذلك، وعن أي أضرار ناجمة عن ذلك.

31.4 Rewrite the following Arabic translation in your own words, without distorting the meaning of the text. Please keep key legal terminologies.

يتمتع الطرف الثاني خلال فترة العقد بجميع الامتيازات و الحقوق التي اعترف بها قانون العمل و التي تنطبق على جميع موظفي الطرف الأول.

المادة السادسة: مسؤولية الطرف الثاني تجاه الطرف الأول

على الطرف الثاني تحمل مسؤولية سلوكه و تصرفه المهني تجاه الطرف الأول واحترام الأوامر والإرشادات التي يتلقاها خلال سير عمله. كما عليه تحمل مسؤولية سلوكه الأخلاقي و المعنوي و مراقبة قوانين و لوائح و عادات و تقاليد البلاد.

المادة السابعة:

على الطرف الثاني أن لا يلاحق أي عمل آخر أو نشاطات لمصلحة جهة أخرى أو لمصلحته الخاصة غير الأعمال المنصوص عليه من قبل عقده مع الشركة العربية للمأكولات.

المادة الثامنة:

على الطرف الثاني احترام اللوائح الداخلية إلى وضعها الطرف الأول والتي أقرتها السلطات المختصة وفقا للقانون.

المادة التاسعة:

يجب تطبيق جميع أحكام قانون العمل الحالي في جميع الحالات و على جميع المواضيع الغير مذكورة جليا في العقد.

المادة العاشرة:

تم إبرام هذا العقد باللغتين العربية و الانجليزية واحتفظ الطرفان بنسخة و ذلك بعد توقيعه وقراءته.

....
....
....
....
....
....
....
....
....
....
....
....
....
....
....
....
....
....

31.5 Identify the major grammatical errors in the following Arabic translation. Then replace the underlined words with appropriate synonyms without distorting the meaning of the text.

وعندما يفضي نزاع ما إلى القتال، كان <u>شغل المجلس الشاغل</u> إنهاء ذلك في أقرب وقت ممكن. وفي مناسبات عديدة، أصدر المجلس تعليمات <u>لوقف إطلاق النار</u> كان لها أهمية حاسمة في <u>الحيلولة</u> دون اتساع رقعة اقتتال. وهو يوفد أيضا قوات الأمم المتحدة لحفظ السلام للمساعدة على <u>تخفيف التوتر</u> في مناطق الاضطرابات، والفصل بين القوات <u>المتحاربة</u> وتهيئة ظروف الهدوء التي يمكن أن يجري في ظلها البحث عن تسويات سلمية. ويجوز للمجلس أن يقرر <u>اتخاذ تدابير</u> إنفاذ، أو جزاءات اقتصادية (مثل عمليات الحظر التجاري) أو اتخاذ إجراء عسكري جماعي.

وعندما يتخذ مجلس الأمن <u>إجراء</u> منع أو إنفاذ ضد دولة عضو ما، يجوز للجمعية العامة، أن <u>تعلق تمتع</u> تلك الدولة بحقوق العضوية <u>وامتيازها</u>، بناء على توصية المجلس. وإذا كررت <u>انتهاكات</u> دولة عضو ما لمبادئ الميثاق، يجوز للجمعية العامة أن تقصيها من الأمم المتحدة، بناء على توصية المجلس.

ويجوز الدولة العضو في الأمم المتحدة التي ليست عضوا في مجلس الأمن، أن تشارك في مناقشات المجلس، بدون حق التصويت، إذا اعتبر هذه الأخير أن مصالحها <u>عرضة</u> للضرر. ويُدعى كل من أعضاء الأمم المتحدة وغير الأعضاء، إذا كانوا أطرافا في نزاع <u>معروض</u> على المجلس، إلى المشاركة في مناقشاته، بدون حق التصويت؛ ويضع المجلس شروطا مشاركة الدولة غير العضو.

....

....

....

....

....

....

....

....

....

....

....

....

....

....

LESSON 32: TRANSLATING AGREEMENTS AND CONTRACTS

The process of translating agreements and contracts is fraught with many challenges, some of which are to do with the specific nature of the material to be translated. Translating agreements and contracts requires a specific knowledge of the subject area, especially since this type of register has a very formal style and tone. Such knowledge could be achieved through the accumulation of vocabulary or glossaries related to this genre of texts.

Therefore, the translator is required not only to have a broad knowledge of the source text, but also a sound knowledge of the TT, especially the equivalent terminologies in it. A good grounding in both languages does not only help in preserving the meaning of the ST, but can also contribute to producing an accurate and reliable translation.

 32.1 *Provide a summary for the following text in Arabic.*

http://www.britishirishcouncil.org/agreement-reached-multi-party-negotiations/strand-3-british-irish-council-and-intergovernmental

BRITISH-IRISH COUNCIL
1. A British-Irish Council (BIC) will be established under a new British-Irish Agreement to promote the harmonious and mutually beneficial development of the totality of relationships among the peoples of these islands.
2. Membership of the BIC will comprise representatives of the British and Irish Governments, devolved institutions in Northern Ireland, Scotland and Wales, when established, and, if appropriate, elsewhere in the United Kingdom, together with representatives of the Isle of Man and the Channel Islands.
3. The BIC will meet in different formats: at summit level, twice per year; in specific sectoral formats on a regular basis, with each side represented by the appropriate Minister; in an appropriate format to consider cross-sectoral matters.
4. Representatives of members will operate in accordance with whatever procedures for democratic authority and accountability are in force in their respective elected institutions.
5. The BIC will exchange information, discuss, consult and use best endeavours to reach agreement on co-operation on matters of mutual interest within the competence of the relevant Administrations. Suitable issues for early discussion in the BIC could include transport links, agricultural issues, environmental issues, cultural issues, health issues, education issues and approaches to EU issues. Suitable arrangements to be made for practical co-operation on agreed policies.
6. It will be open to the BIC to agree common policies or common actions.

Individual members may opt not to participate in such common policies and common action.

7. The BIC normally will operate by consensus. In relation to decisions on common policies or common actions, including their means of implementation, it will operate by agreement of all members participating in such policies or actions.

(accessed 14 April 2013)

....
....
....
....
....
....
....
....
....
....
....
....
....
....
....
....
....

32.2 *Provide the Arabic equivalents of the underlined English words/phrases in the following text and use them in sentences.*

1. A British-Irish Council (BIC) will be established under a new British-Irish Agreement to promote the harmonious and <u>mutually beneficial development</u> of the totality of relationships among the peoples of these islands.

2. Membership of the BIC will <u>comprise</u> representatives of the British and Irish Governments, <u>devolved institutions</u> in Northern Ireland, Scotland and Wales, when

established, and, if appropriate, elsewhere in the United Kingdom, together with representatives of the Isle of Man and the Channel Islands.

3. The BIC will meet in different formats: at summit level, twice per year; in specific sectoral formats on a regular basis, with each side represented by the appropriate Minister; in an appropriate format to consider cross-sectoral matters.

4. Representatives of members will operate in accordance with whatever procedures for democratic authority and accountability are in force in their respective elected institutions.

5. The BIC will exchange information, discuss, consult and use best endeavours to reach agreement on co-operation on matters of mutual interest within the competence of the relevant Administrations. Suitable issues for early discussion in the BIC could include transport links, agricultural issues, environmental issues, cultural issues, health issues, education issues and approaches to EU issues. Suitable arrangements to be made for practical co-operation on agreed policies.

http://www.britishirishcouncil.org/agreement-reached-multi-party-negotiations/strand-3-british-irish-council-and-intergovernmental (accessed 14 April 2013)

32.3 *Provide two antonyms in Arabic for each underlined English word/phrase.*

The British Government will <u>complete</u> incorporation into Northern Ireland law of the European Convention on Human Rights (ECHR), with direct access to the courts, and <u>remedies</u> for <u>breach</u> of the Convention, including power for the courts to <u>overrule</u> Assembly legislation <u>on grounds</u> of inconsistency.

<u>Subject to</u> the outcome of public consultation underway, the British Government <u>intends</u>, as a particular <u>priority</u>, to create a statutory obligation on public authorities in Northern Ireland to <u>carry out</u> all their functions with due regard to the need <u>to promote</u> equality of opportunity in relation to religion and political opinion; gender; race; disability; age; marital status; dependants; and <u>sexual orientation</u>. Public bodies would be required <u>to draw up</u> statutory schemes showing how they would implement this obligation. Such schemes would cover <u>arrangements</u> for policy <u>appraisal</u>, including an <u>assessment of impact</u> on relevant categories, public consultation, public access to information and services, <u>monitoring</u> and timetables.

https://peaceaccords.nd.edu/matrix/status/6/human_rights (accessed 7 August 2013)

....

....

....

....

....

....

....

....

....

....

....

....

....

....

....

32.4 *Provide two main titles in Arabic for the following text.*

The Irish Government will also take steps to further strengthen the protection of human rights in its jurisdiction. The Government will, taking account of the work of the All-Party Oireacht as Committee on the Constitution and the Report of the Constitution Review Group, bring forward measures to strengthen and underpin the constitutional protection of human rights. These proposals will draw on the European Convention on Human Rights and other international legal instruments in the field of human rights and the question of the incorporation of the ECHR will be further examined in this context. The measures brought forward would ensure at least an equivalent level of protection of human rights as will pertain in Northern Ireland.

https://peaceaccords.nd.edu/matrix/status/6/human_rights (accessed 7 August 2013)

1. ....

2. ....

 32.5 *Translate the following paragraphs into Arabic, paying special attention to the translation of negation.*

Tenancy Obligations

Tenants must:

- pay the rent and any other specified charges
- avoid causing or make good any damage beyond normal wear and tear
- notify the landlord of any repair requirements
- allow access for repairs to be carried out and by appointment for routine inspections
- keep the landlord informed of the identity of the occupants
- not engage in or allow anti-social behaviour
- not act, or allow visitors to act in a way that would invalidate the landlord's insurance
- not cause the landlord to be in breach of statutory obligations
- not alter, improve, assign, sub-let or change the use of the dwelling without written consent from the landlord.

Landlords must:

- allow the tenant to enjoy peaceful and exclusive occupation
- carry out repairs, subject to tenant liability for damage beyond normal wear and tear
- insure the dwelling, subject to the insurance being available at a reasonable cost
- provide a point of contact
- promptly refund deposits unless rent is owing or there is damage beyond normal wear and tear
- reimburse tenants for expenditure on repairs that were appropriate to the landlord
- enforce tenant obligations
- not penalise tenants for making complaints or taking action to enforce their rights.

LESSON 33: SECURITY COUNCIL: TERMS AND CONDITIONS AND PEACE AGREEMENTS

One of the immediate challenges to translators when translating this genre of text is the need for a sound knowledge of current political affairs, as well as the historical factors governing these agreements. A good knowledge of the conflict and the parties involved are crucial to a balanced and representative translation. Familiarity with key agreement terminologies is vital for a successful translation. Glossaries as well as the familiarity with the United Nations formalities and register could help in overcoming any problems which might rise as a consequence of the complexity of the glossary related to the above genre.

Again, a glossary of key terminologies and phrases in both Arabic and English could assist in providing a clear and reliable translation.

33.1 *Provide synonyms and antonyms in Arabic for the underlined Arabic words and phrases below. Then comment on the strategies used in the Arabic translation.*

Article 39
The Security Council shall determine the existence of any threat to the peace, breach of the peace, or act of aggression and shall make recommendations, or decide what measures shall be taken in accordance with Articles 41 and 42, to maintain or restore international peace and security.

Article 40
In order to prevent an aggravation of the situation, the Security Council may before making the recommendations or deciding upon the measures provided for in Article 39, call upon the parties concerned to comply with such provisional measures as it deems necessary or desirable. Such provisional measures shall be without prejudice to the rights, claims, or position of the parties concerned. The Security Council shall duly take account of failure to comply with such provisional measures.

Arabic translation

المادة 39
يقرر مجلس الأمن ما إذا كان قد وقع تهديد للسلم أو إخلال به أو كان ما وقع عملا من أعمال العدوان، ويقدم في ذلك توصياته أو يقرر ما يجب اتخاذه من التدابير طبقا لأحكام المادتين 41 و 42 لحفظ السلم والأمن الدولي أو إعادته إلى نصابه.

المادة 40
منعاً لتفاقم الموقف، لمجلس الأمن، قبل أن يقدم توصياته أو يتخذ التدابير المنصوص عليها في المادة 39 ، أن يدعو المتنازعين للأخذ بما يراه ضرورياً أو مستحسناً من تدابير مؤقتة، ولا تخلّ هذه التدابير المؤقتة بحقوق المتنازعين ومطالبهم أو بمركزهم، وعلى مجلس الأمن أن يحسب لعدم أخذ المتنازعين بهذه التدابير المؤقتة حسابه.

....

....

....

....

....

....

....

....

....

33.2 *Identify and correct the errors in the Arabic translation of the following English text.*

Article 41

The Security Council may decide what measures not involving the use of armed force are to be employed to give effect to its decisions, and it may call upon the Members of the United Nations to apply such measures. These may include complete or partial interruption of economic relations and of rail, sea, air, postal, telegraphic, radio, and other means of communication, and the severance of diplomatic relations.

Article 42

Should the Security Council consider that measures provided for in Article 41 would be inadequate or have proved to be inadequate, it may take such action by air, sea, or land forces as may be necessary to maintain or restore international peace and security. Such action may include demonstrations, blockade, and other operations by air, sea, or land forces of Members of the United Nations.

Arabic translation

المادة 41

لمجلس الأمن أن يقرر ما يجب أخذه من التدابير التي لا تتطلب مستخدم القوات المسلحة تنفيذا لقراراته، وله أن يطلب إلى أعضاء "الأمم المتحدة" تطبيق هذه تدابير، ويجوز أن يكون من بينها وقف صلات الاقتصادية والمواصلات الحديدية والبحرية والبريدية والبرقية واللاسلكية وغيرها من وسائل المواصلات وقفا كليا وقطع العلاقات دبلوماسية.

المادة 42

إذا يرى مجلس الأمن أن تدابير الموجودة في المادة 41 لا تفي بالغرض أو ثبت أنها لم تف به، جاز له أن يتخذ بطريق القوات الجوية والبحرية والبرية من الأعمال ما يلزم لحفظ السلم والأمن الدولي أو لإعادتها إلى نصابها. ويجوز أن تتناول هذه الأعمال المظاهرات والحصر والعمليات الأخرى بطريق القوات الجوية أو البحرية التابع لأعضاء الأمم المتحدة.

....

....

....

....

....

....

....

....

....

33.3 *Replace the underlined words in the following text with appropriate synonyms.*

<u>قواعد عمومية</u>

مادة -:1
تسرى أحكام هذا القانون على كل من <u>يرتكب</u> في القطر المصري جريمة من الجرائم <u>المنصوص عليها</u> فيه.

مادة -:2
تسرى أحكام هذا القانون أيضا على الأشخاص الآتي ذكرهم:

أولا: كل من ارتكب في خارج <u>القطر</u> فعلا يجعله فاعلا أو شريكا في جريمة <u>وقعت</u> كلها أو بعضها في القطر المصري.

ثانيا: كل من ارتكب في خارج القطر جريمة من الجرائم الآتية:

أ) جناية <u>مخلة</u> بأمن الحكومة مما نص عليه في البابين الأول والثاني من الكتاب الثاني من هذا القانون.

ب) جناية تزوير مما نص عليه في المادة 206 من هذا القانون .

ج) (1) جناية تقليد أو تزيف أو تزوير عملة ورقية أو معدنية مما نص عليه في المادة 202 أو جناية إدخال تلك العملة الورقية أو المعدنية المقلدة أو <u>المزيفة</u> أو المزورة إلى مصر أو إخراجها منها أو ترويجها أو <u>حيازتها بقصد الترويج</u> أو التعامل بها مما نص علية في المادة 203 بشرط أن تكون العملة متداولة قانونا في مصر .

مادة -:3
كل مصري ارتكب وهو في خارج القطر فعلا يعتبر جناية

(1) البند(ج) من المادة 2 استبدل بموجب القانون رقم 68 لسنة 1956. أو <u>جنحة</u> في هذا القانون يعاقب <u>بمقتضى</u> أحكامه إذا عاد إلى القطر وكان الفعل معاقبا عليه بمقتضى قانون البلد الذي ارتكبه فيه.

مادة -:4
لا تقام الدعوى العمومية على مرتكب جريمة أو فعل في الخارج إلا من النيابة العمومية .

ولا تجوز إقامتها على من يثبت أن المحاكم الأجنبية <u>برأته</u> مما <u>أسند إليه</u> أو أنها حكمت عليه نهائيا واستوفى عقوبته.

مادة -:5
يعاقب على الجرائم بمقتضى القانون <u>المعمول به</u> وقت ارتكابها.

ومع هذا إذا صدر بعد وقوع الفعل وقبل الحكم فيه نهائيا قانون أصلح للمتهم فهو الذي يتبع دون غيره.

وإذا صدر قانون بعد حكم نهائي يجعل الفعل الذي حكم على المجرم من اجله غير معاقب عليه يوقف تنفيذ الحكم وتنتهي آثاره الجنائية .

غير انه في حالة قيام إجراءات الدعوى أو <u>صدور</u> حكم بالإدانة فيها وكان ذلك عن فعل وقع مخالفا للقانون ينهى عن ارتكبه في فترة محدودة فان انتهاء هذه الفترة <u>لا يحول دون</u> السير في الدعوى أو تنفيذ العقوبات المحكوم بها.

<u>مادة -:6</u>
لا يمس الحكم بالعقوبات المنصوص عليها في القانون ما يكون واجبا للخصوم من الرد والتعويض.

<u>مادة -: 7</u>
لا تخل أحكام هذا القانون في أي حال من الأحوال بحقوق الشخصية المقررة في الشريعة <u>الغراء.</u>

<u>مادة -:8</u>
تراعى أحكام الكتاب الأول من هذا القانون في الجرائم <u>المنصوص</u> عليها في القوانين واللوائح الخصوصية إلا إذا وجد فيها نص <u>يخالف ذلك.</u>

http://www.aladalacenter.com/index.php?option=com_content&view=article&id=476:
2009-03-27-19-08-08&catid=76:2009-02-06-21-54-53&Itemid=90 (accessed
10 February 2013)

33.4 *Translate the following Arabic text into English.*

كوفي عنان يدعو لاصلاح مجلس الامن الدولي ويرى ضرورة لمشاركة ايران في "جنيف-2"

15.07.2013

أعرب كوفي عنان الأمين العام السابق للأمم المتحدة عن قناعته بضرورة اصلاح مجلس الامن الدولي، مشيرا الى أن شكله الحالي يعكس الوضع الجيوسياسي الذي كان في تسعينات القرن الماضي.

ولفت كوفي عنان اثناء حفل تقديمه كتابه الجديد "Interventions: A Life in War and Peace" بموسكو يوم الاثنين 15 يوليو/تموز، لفت الانتباه الى ان الهند التي يبلغ عدد سكانها مليار نسمة، ليس لها مقعد في مجلس الأمن. كما اشار الى عدم وجود تمثيل لافريقيا وامريكا اللاتينية في المجلس.

وتطرق كوفي عنان الذي كان ايضا مبعوثا خاصا للأمم المتحدة والجامعة العربية الى سورية، تطرق الى موضوع الأزمة السورية ودعا الى عدم تحميل الأمم المتحدة المسؤولية الكاملة عن الوضع في سورية. وقال ان كل شيء يتوقف على الدول الأعضاء النافذة في الأمم المتحدة.

واشار المبعوث الدولي السابق الى ان المعارضة السورية متشتتة سياسيا وعسكريا، واضاف ان "القوى الدولية تعمل في المنطقة مع مجموعات محددة، ولكن يجب بذل الكثير من الجهود لتوحيد المعارضة. واعرب عن اعتقاده بان مجلس الامن الدولي لا يمكن ان يلعب دورا فعالا في تسوية الازمة السورية، إلا في حال تحدث بصوت واحد.

واعرب كوفي عنان عن أمله بأن يعقد مؤتمر "جنيف-2" حول سورية بأسرع ما يمكن، وان تتمكن الدول من التوصل الى الاتفاق بهذا الشأن. وشدد على ان ايران يجب ان تكون أحد الاطراف المشاركة في اتخاذ القرار.

والجدير بالذكر ان مسألة مشاركة ايران في المؤتمر الدولي المرتقب تثير خلافات بين روسيا التي تصر على ضرورة دعوة ايران، والولايات المتحدة التي تعارض ذلك.

http://arabic.rt.com/news/621190 (accessed 22 July 2013)

....

....

....

....

....

....

....

....

....

....

....

....

....

....

....

....

....

....

....

....

....

....

....

....

....

33.5 *Summarise the following Arabic text in three main headings.*

أشار المبعوث الخاص للأمم المتحدة الى العراق مارتن كوبلر الى ان التوترات السياسية الداخلية بالاضافة الى تداعيات الأزمة السورية هي السبب في احتدام وتيرة العنف في العراق.

وحذر كوبلر متحدثا امام مجلس الامن الدولي الثلاثاء 16 يوليو/ تموز، من ان العنف المتزايد في العراق، والذي أدى الى سقوط حوالي 3 الآف قتيل واكثر من 7 الآف جريح في غضون الاربعة أشهر الاخيرة، يهدد هذا البلد بسلوك "طريق خطر".

وأكد المسؤول الاممي، الذي تسلم منصبه مؤخرا، ان الزعماء العراقيين يواجهون "خيارات حاسمة"، فهم اما ان يختاروا "تعزيز أسس الديموقراطية" او ان يختاروا "المغامرة بسلوك طريق خطر حيث تنتظرهم المآزق السياسية واعمال العنف الطائفية عند كل مفترق طرق".

وأضاف كوبلر ان الخبراء يعتبرون ان المتمردين يحاولون الاستفادة من مشاعر الاستياء لدى الاقلية السنية التي تشعر بانها "مستهدفة" من الحكومة التي يهيمن عليها الشيعة في العراق.

وشدد أيضا على ضرورة معالجة أسباب الصراع في العراق وايجاد حل سياسي للحرب الأهلية في سورية المجاورة، مبينا ان الصراعات في العراق وسورية تتداخل وأن الجماعات المسلحة العراقية أصبح لها وجود فعال على نحو متزايد في سورية.

وقال انه نتيجة لذلك : لم يعد الصراع السوري مجرد امتداد لما يحدث في العراق، ولكن وبحسب ما وردنا فان العراقيين يحملون السلاح ضد بعضهم البعض داخل سورية.

http://arabic.rt.com/news/621371 (accessed 22 July 2013)

1. ....

2. ....

3. ....

MODULE REVIEW EXERCISES

1. *Provide antonyms for the underlined words in the following text.*

لائحة بأهم القوانين المصرفية

والمالية الصادرة منذ منتصف القرن الماضي

- **قانون سرّية المصارف الصادر بتاريخ 1956/9/3:** إن مديري ومستخدمي المصارف ملزمون بكتمان السرّ المصرفي كتماناً مطلقاً لمصلحة زبائن المصرف وعدم إفشاء أسماء الزبائن وأموالهم والمعطيات المتعلّقة بهم لأيّ شخص أو سلطة عامة إدارية أو عسكرية أو قضائية؛ إمكانية فتح حسابات وودائع مرقّمة.

- **قانون إجازة فتح حساب مشترك الصادر بتاريخ 1691/12/19:** يمكن للمصارف أن تفتح لزبائنها حساباً مشتركاً يُستعمل بتوقيع أحد أصحاب هذا الحساب منفرداً. عند وفاة أحد أصحاب الحساب المشترك يتصرّف الشريك والشركاء بكامل الحساب مطلق التصرّف.

- **قانون النقد والتسليف الصادر بالمرسوم رقم 31531 في 1963/8/1:** هذا القانون هو الركيزة الأساسية للجهاز المصرفي والمالي إذ يرعى تنظيم النقد ودور المصرف المركزي وعملياته، وينظّم عمل المصارف إضافة الى المهن التابعة للمهنة المصرفية.

- **القانون رقم 67/28** الذي عدّل بعض أحكام قانون النقد والتسليف، وأنشأ لدى مصرف لبنان لجنة مستقلة تقوم بمراقبة صارمة ودائمة لمجمل النشاط المصرفي هي **لجنة الرقابة على المصارف.** وأسّس **المؤسسة الوطنية لضمان الودائع** ، كما أن المادة 54 منه أوقفت لمدة خمس سنوات قابلة التمديد الترخيص لمصارف جديدة.

- **المرسوم رقم 1968/11564:** تصديق النظام الأساسي للمؤسسة الوطنية لضمان الودائع.

- **المرسوم رقم 1971/1983:** تنظيم مهنة مفوّضي الرقابة لدى المصارف.

- **القانون الموضوع موضع التنفيذ بالمرسوم رقم 1973/6102** : الذي عدّل بعض أحكام قانون النقد والتسليف وتضمّن تعديلات تهدف بصورة خاصة إلى إزالة القيود غير المبرّرة التي تعيق ممارسة المهنة أو تضيّق مجالات الاستثمار. وطالت التعديلات المواد رقم 76، 102، 105، 152، 153، 186 من هذا القانون. أما المادة 471 الجديدة، فقد نصّت على وجوب استطلاع رأي جمعية مصارف لبنان عندما يضع مصرف لبنان التنظيمات العامة المصرفية.

http://www.imarwaiktissad.com/docs/mahalyat/mahalyat12.html (accessed 7 November 2013)

....

....

....

....

....

....

....

206

....
....
....
....
....
....
....
....

2. Translate and comment on the grammatical difference between the ST and TT at both the sentence and discourse levels.

1. The WTO shall provide the common institutional framework for the conduct of trade relations among its Members in matters related to the agreements and associated legal instruments included in the Annexes to this Agreement.
2. The agreements and associated legal instruments included in Annexes 1, 2, and 3 (hereinafter referred to as 'Multilateral Trade Agreements') are integral parts of this Agreement, binding on all Members.
3. The agreements and associated legal instruments included in Annex 4 (hereinafter referred to as 'Plurilateral Trade Agreements') are also part of this Agreement for those Members that have accepted them, and are binding on those Members. The Plurilateral Trade Agreements do not create either obligations or rights for Members that have not accepted them.
4. The General Agreement on Tariffs and Trade 1994 as specified in Annex 1A (hereinafter referred to as 'GATT 1994') is legally distinct from the General Agreement on Tariffs and Trade, dated 30 October 1947, annexed to the Final Act Adopted at the Conclusion of the Second Session of the Preparatory Committee of the United Nations Conference on Trade and Employment, as subsequently rectified, amended or modified (hereinafter referred to as 'GATT 1947').

http://www.wto.org/english/docs_e/legal_e/04-wto_e.htm (accessed 5 November 2012)

....
....
....
....
....
....
....
....

....

....

....

....

....

....

....

....

....

....

....

....

3. *Provide a summary in Arabic for the following text. Then comment on the translation difficulties you encountered at both the sentence and discourse levels.*

RENT. Resident shall pay to Owner the Monthly rent of $ ......, in advance on or before the first day of each month without deduction or offset. On signing this Agreement Resident shall pay one full month's rent in the form of a cashier's check or money order only. The rent for the partial month's prior shall be prorated on the basis of a 30-day month and shall be paid on or before the next rental due date.

SECURITY DEPOSIT. On signing this Agreement, Resident shall pay to Owner the sum of $ ...... as a deposit to secure resident's performance of the covenants contained herein. No part of this deposit is to be considered as an advance payment of rent, including last months' rent, nor is it to be used for refunded prior to the leased premises being permanently and totally vacated by all Residents. After Resident has vacated the premises, Owner shall furnish Resident with an itemized written statement of the basis for, and the amount of, any of the security deposit retained by Owner. Owner may withhold that portion of Resident's security deposit necessary (a) to remedy any default by Resident in the payment of rent or any other provision of this Agreement, (b) to repair damages to the premises, to include repainting, but exclusive of ordinary wear and tear, and (c) to remove trash and clean the premises to meet Owner's re-rental standards, as provided by law. The unused portion of this deposit shall be returned to Resident without interest, according to law.

http://www.westsiderentals.com/pdf/rental_agreement.pdf (accessed 30 September 2012)

....

....

....
....
....
....
....
....
....
....
....
....
....
....
....
....
....
....
....
....
....

| 4. *Translate the above text using the communicative translation strategy* | ⟳ |

....
....
....
....
....
....
....
....
....
....
....

....

....

....

....

....

....

....

....

....

5. Translate the following text into English.

- **القانون رقم 67/28** الذي عدّل بعض أحكام قانون النقد والتسليف، وأنشأ لدى مصرف لبنان لجنة مستقلة تقوم بمراقبة صارمة ودائمة لمجمل النشاط المصرفي هي **لجنة الرقابة على المصارف**. وأسّس **المؤسسة الوطنية لضمان الودائع**، كما أن المادة 54 منه أوقفت لمدة خمس سنوات قابلة التمديد الترخيص لمصارف جديدة.

- **المرسوم رقم 1968/11564:** تصديق النظام الأساسي للمؤسسة الوطنية لضمان الودائع.

- **المرسوم رقم 1971/1983:** تنظيم مهنة مفوّضي الرقابة لدى المصارف.

- **القانون الموضوع موضع التنفيذ بالمرسوم رقم 1973/6102 :** الذي عدّل بعض أحكام قانون النقد والتسليف وتضمّن تعديلات تهدف بصورة خاصة إلى إزالة القيود غير المبرّرة التي تعيق ممارسة المهنة أو تضيّق مجالات الاستثمار. وطالت التعديلات المواد رقم 76، 102، 105، 152، 153، 186 من هذا القانون. أما المادة 174 الجديدة، فقد نصّت على وجوب استطلاع رأي جمعية مصارف لبنان عندما يضع مصرف لبنان التنظيمات العامة المصرفية.

....

....

....

....

....

....

....

....

....

Bibliography

Alcaraz, Enrique and Brian Hughes (2002), *Translation Practices Explained, Legal Translation Explained*, Manchester: St. Jerome.

Amigoni, David (2000), *The English Novel and Prose Narrative: Elements of literature*, Edinburgh: Edinburgh University Press.

Baker, Mona (1987), 'Review of Methods Used for Coining New Terms in Arabic', *Meta.* 32(2), pp. 186–8.

Baker, Mona (1992), *In Other Words*, London and New York: Routledge.

Baker, Mona And Gabriela Saldanha (eds) (2009), *The Routledge Encyclopedia of Translation Studies* (2nd edn), London and New York: Routledge.

Bal, Mieke (1985), *Narratology: Introduction to the Theory of Narrative*, Toronto: University of Toronto Press.

Bassnett-McGuire, Susan (1980), *Translation Studies*, New York: Methuen & Co. Ltd.

Bassnett-McGuire, Susan (1991a), 'Translating for the Theatre: the Case Against Performability', *TTR.* 4(1), pp. 99–111.

Bassnett-McGuire, Susan (1991b), *Translation Studies* (rev. edn), London and New York: Routledge.

Bastin, Georges (2009), 'Adaptation', in Baker and Saldanha (eds), *The Routledge Encyclopedia of Translation Studies* (2nd edn), London and New York: Routledge, pp. 3–5.

Bell, Allan (1991), *The Language of News Media*, Oxford: Basil Blackwell Ltd.

Bielsa, Esperanca (2009), 'Translation in Global News', *The Translator Studies in Intercultural Communication* 15(1), pp. 135–55.

Byrne, Jody (2006), *Technical Translation: Usability Strategies for Translating Technical Documentation*, Dordrecht: Springer.

Carroll, Lewis (1994) [1865], *Alice's Adventures in Wonderland*, London: Puffin Books.

Conrad, Joseph (1981), *Heart of Darkness and The Secret Sharer* (Bantam Classics), Toronto: Bantam Books.

Conrad, Joseph (1992) [1900], *Lord Jim. A tale* (Everyman's library), London: David Campbell Pub.

Dickens, Charles (1995) [1854], *Hard Times*, Oxford: Heinemann New Windmills.

Dickens, Charles, *The Haunted House* [online]. Available from http://www.eastoftheweb.com/short-stories/UBooks/HaunHous.shtml

Dickins, James (2009), 'Junction in English and Arabic: Syntactic, Discoursal and Denotative Features', *Journal of Pragmatics*, 42, pp. 1076–136.

Dickins, James, Sandor Hervey and Ian Higgins (2002), *Thinking Arabic Translation. A Course in Translation Method: Arabic to English*, London: Routledge.

Dobrzyńska, T. (1995), 'Translating Metaphor: Problems of Meaning', *Journal of Pragmatics*, 24(6), pp. 595–604.

El-Farahaty, Hanem (2011), *Problems of Translating Legal Discourse with Special Reference to the United Nations Documents* (PhD Dissertation), University of Leeds.

Fawcett, Peter (1983), 'Translation modes and constraints', *The Incorporated Linguist*, 22(4), pp. 186–90.

Goodrich, Peter (1987), *Legal Discourse: Studies in Linguistics, Rhetoric and Legal Analysis*, London: Palgrave Macmillan.

Graedler, Anne L. (2000), 'Cultural shock', accessed 6 December 2006 from http://www.hf.uio.no/.../top7culture.html

Greenough, James Bradstreet and George Lyman Kittredge (2001), *Words and Their Ways in English Speech*, New York: Adamant Media Corporation.

Halliday, M. A. K., and Ruqaiya Hasan (1976), *Cohesion in English*, London: Longman.

Harvey, Malcolm (2000), 'A Beginner's Course in Legal Translation: the Case of Culture-bound Terms', *Journal of Pragmatics* [online], 24, pp. 595–604. Available from http://www.tradulex.org/Actes2000/harvey.pdf

Hemingway, Ernest (2000) [1952], *The Old Man and the Sea*, London: Vintage.

Henderson, Willie (1982), 'Metaphor in Economics' in *Economics*, 18(4), pp. 147–57.

Hervey, Sándor and Ian Higgins (1992), *Thinking Translation. A Course in Translation Method: French to English*, London: Routledge.

Hiltunen, Risto (1990), *Chapters on Legal English: Aspects Past and Present of the Language of the Law*, Helsinki: Suomalainen Tiedeakatemia.

Ivir Vladimir (1987), 'Procedures and strategies for the translation of culture', in Gideon Toury (ed.), *Translation across cultures*, New Delhi: Bahri Publications, pp. 36–48.

Katamba, Francis (2004), *English Words: Structure, History, Usage*, Abingdon: Routledge.

Labov, William (1972), *Language in the Inner City*, Philadelphia: University of Pennsylvania Press.

Larson, Mildred L. (1984/1998), *Meaning-based translation: a guide to cross-language equivalence*, Lanham: University Press of America.

Newmark, Peter (1982), 'The Translation of Authoritative Statements: A Discussion', *Meta*, vol. XXVII (4), pp. 375–91.

Newmark, Peter (1988a), *A textbook of translation*, New York: Prentice Hall.

Newmark, Peter (1988b), *Approaches to translation*, Hertfordshire: Prentice Hall.

Pinchuck, Isadore (1977), *Scientific and technical translation*, London: A. Deutsch.

Reah, Danuta (2002), *The Language of Newspapers* (2nd edn), Routledge.

Rowland, Dominic and Simon Avery (2001), 'Styles of Journalism' in *Writing with Style*, ed. Rebecca Stott and Simon Avery, London: Longman Group Ltd, pp. 105–26.

Sager, Juan C. (1993), *Language Engineering and Translation*, Amsterdam/Philadelphia: Benjamins.

Šarčević, Susan (1997), *New Approach to Legal Translation*, London/Boston: Kluwer Law International.

Schwartz, H. (2012), 'Legal and administrative language', *Vidas intraducibles* [online], adapted from T.P. Beatriz Sosa and T.P. Mercedes Ugarte (1977), 'Legal and administrative language', *Babel* 25(1). Available from http://vidasintraducibles.blogspot.com/2011/09/legal-and-administrative-language.html (accessed 1 January 2013)

Stross, Charles (1997), *A Colder War*, Infinity Plus [online]. Available from http://www.infinityplus.co.uk/stories/colderwar.htm

Thorne, Sara (1997), *Advanced English Language*, New York: Palgrave.

Venuti, Lawrence (1995), *The Translator's Invisibility: A History of Translation*, London and New York: Routledge.

Venuti, Lawrence (2008), *The Translator's Invisibility: A History of Translation*, New York: Routledge.

Verdonk, Peter (2002), *Stylistics*, Oxford: Oxford University Press.

Vinay, Jean-Paul and Jean Darbelnet (1958/1995), *Comparative stylistics of French and English: a methodology for translation*, trans. and ed. Juan C. Sager and Marie-Jo Hamel (1995), Amsterdam and Philadelphia: John Benjamins. Originally published as *Stylistique comparée du français et de l'anglais: Méthode de traduction*, Paris: Didier.